*Dedicated to all the
talented writers who dream
of seeing their work in print.
Our goal is to transform their
dreams into reality.*

Table of Contents

Table of Contents

Introduction

Who Speaks for the Heartland?

There is a long literary tradition of writers using prefaces to explicate and justify breakthrough moments in poetry and prose. In the second edition of *Lyrical Ballads* (the first edition having received considerable critical drubbing), Wordsworth wrote a long preface to explain just what he and Coleridge thought they were doing. Thereafter, the poetry was much more favorably received. In the early days of the twentieth century, Elkin Matthews, the editor of the Georgian Poetry series, added a "prefatory note" to the first edition to announce his belief that they stood on the threshold of a new era of poetry, one "which may rank in due time with the several great poetic eras of the past." The problem with such a proclamation, of course, is that you never really know whether you are on the threshold of a new era, or simply whistling wistfully in a literary back alley. If my lifelong study of literature has taught me anything, however, it is that when the world is ready for, indeed, needs, a new literary movement, one will arise. Today, the need clearly exists. The only question is what form the movement will take. So consider this preface not so much an announcement as a prediction: The next movement in American letters will emerge not from academia, not from critical circles, and not from New York. It will come from the heartland.

For far too long, the voices of the heartland have suffered from a massive cultural inferiority complex. It's not entirely our fault—this point of view is constantly reinforced by the media, by academia, by critics, by the multitude of voices trying to tell us what art matters and what art doesn't. To hear some people talk, everything important is taking place…somewhere else. On one coast or the other. Not here in "flyover country." Is this justified? The great American writers may have been published in New York, or written screenplays in L.A., but how many of them actually lived there? No, the vibrant, new, living voices come from the heartland, then, now, and always. To see your subject without the jaded and jaundiced perspective of one who has seen too much, who thinks all the great stories have already been told, that's the true challenge. Writing the same old same old might be safer. But it isn't writing from the heart.

Unquestionably, the old borders, the artificial barriers that have been erected between one kind of book and another, are crumbling, washing away like silt in a heavy rain. These borders have not always been with us. Not until the turn of the twentieth century, with the advent of "English" being taught in English-speaking universities as a study of literature, not the language, did we see the emergence of the modern-day dichotomy between serious fiction and popular, between literary fiction and genre. This bifurcation of books served a purpose in academia and, it must be said, in the marketplace. That identifying label on the spine tells the barely-read teen toiling at Barnes & Noble where to shelve the book. But it serves little purpose for writers, who have always chafed and struggled against the need to pigeonhole their work as one thing or another, especially given the presumption that some categories are inherently more important than others. Pulitzer Prize-winner Michael Chabon has written eloquently of the arrogance of the assumption that only the literary story, the "largely plotless, character-driven, moment-of-epiphany" literary tale is of merit. In response, he has proposed a blurring of the borders, what he calls "trickster fiction," a melding of literary and genre fictions designed not to placate critics or booksellers but to allow writers to achieve their own artistic goals. My own preference would be not so much to blur the borders as to demolish them with a two-megaton nuclear device and then use CIA brainwashing techniques to make the world forget they ever existed. True, writing must take some form, but that form should be an outgrowth of the work and the writer working, not an artificial construct imposed by forces alien to the creative process.

Which leads to this anthology. The purpose of the Heartland Writers Workshop, as well as the call for submissions that resulted in this book, and for that matter, the sponsoring entity, HAWK Publishing, is first and foremost to create a forum for new voices, but also to allow those voices to express themselves without the influence and predisposition inherent in any academic or commercial competition. Many of these authors, I believe, will go on to write other and better things, to find a place for themselves in the world of letters. Whether they do or do not, however, for this moment in time, these writers of the heartland are speaking from the heart.

In the early nineteenth century, in his *Biographia Literaria*, Coleridge implored his fellow poets to "Make it real." A century later, Ezra Pound urged his modernist colleagues to "Make it new." Well, another hundred years have passed. It's time for a new directive, so here it is: Make it true. Now more than ever, we need writers who have the ability to see from the inside out, to convey what Faulkner called "the human heart in conflict with itself." We can do this, and because we can, we must. Ultimately, the "heartland" is not simply a geographic designation; when I speak of voices from the heartland, I mean the emotional heart, the psychological center of gravity around which our lives revolve—the place where all good stories live, where they happen, where they are true. That is the ultimate objective for a heartland writer: to transcend the artificial boundaries and portray the inner workings of the human heart.

William Bernhardt
Founder & President of HAWK Publishing Group, Inc.

Death Keeper
by
M. Carolyn Steele

The old man wakes knowing—knowing death walked on silent feet again, much as it had every night for weeks. Maybe the soft hoot of the owl in the near distance had alerted him. Maybe, though, it was the sure knowledge that death was a hungry master, its appetite never satisfied, guarding each soul closely, waiting.

The owl, death's messenger, hoots again, closer. With a sigh, the old man struggles to sit, allowing his frost-crusted blanket to fall away, allowing the cold night air to embrace him. He wraps strips of fabric holding threadbare moccasins to his feet.

Bones pop and crackle like brittle tree limbs as he rises. The pain does not matter. Pain reminds that he is alive and has to hurry. It would not do for the soldiers to find death's victim first. Bodies piled in wagons, dumped without ceremony or left in gullies for the wolves that trail the forced march from Georgia.

Campfires glitter in the darkness as far as he can see in either direction. The fires of several thousand Creeks trying desperately to hold back the cold, make it through another night so tomorrow they can shuffle and crawl ever closer to the promised land—Indian Territory. Promised. Only a fool believes the land will be Indian for more than a generation. Then the invaders will come again, like ants from an anthill.

He turns, testing the air, sorting the wood smoke from the odor of the white soldier's bitter coffee, a whiff of tobacco, the acrid scent of urine. Which direction? The sweet smell of death rises, churning, growing, drawing him to the east—the direction of home, the direction of the ancestors.

Time is short. The old man secures his only tool, the shoulder blade of a deer, around his waist and pulls a cape of tails—coyote, fox and squirrel—tight across his back. He rolls his few possessions into his blanket, picks a flaming branch from the fire, and starts the hunt.

Light from the torch drapes him in a soft glow, shifting only when he holds it low to examine a prone figure, as he looks for death. Several open their eyes and when they see him, shrink back, eyes wide with fear. No, it is not their time, he assures them and goes on, guided by a sense he would not be able to explain if he cared to.

A wind stirs, clearing the low cloud of smoke, cleansing the air, leaving the cold taste of metal in the old man's mouth. The assortment of tails attached to his cape flutter like they want to flee, want to escape back into the forests.

A soldier, astride a tired roan, patrols the parameters of the camp and pauses. The old man can feel the soldier's glare following him, but does not stop. He knows the rider is warm inside his great coat, knows he doesn't really want to shift his position and allow a finger of cold to crawl up his sleeve. The soldier clucks to his horse and moves away.

So many people, huddled under low brush arbors, in wagons, beside campfires—piled one upon another, living on each other's warmth like parasites. So many, he cannot count them. Hollow-eyed children cough and turn their faces to the ground. Cough is a living thing, traveling from one mouth to another, staying until all breath is gone.

He is close now. He can feel it and stands still, waiting for death to show him the way. Then, he sees it—sees a lump in the shadow of a great hickory. The tree is in mourning, bare branches drooping, keeping a steady beat in the wind, like the drummers of old beating out a message of sorrow.

The lump stirs at his approach. A bony arm flings off the dark blue government issue blanket that covers a thin body.

"Death Keeper," she whispers.

"I am here, old mother," he answers. He pushes a damp strand of hair from her forehead and his fingertips are seared with heat. Her eyes blaze with fever, with the knowledge his presence brings.

"I am ready," she says at last. "It is time." The acceptance seems to bring her peace. She twines her long fingers together, joints swollen like boles on a tree, and carefully places them across her chest. Two beaten silver bracelets gleam in the torchlight against her acorn brown skin.

He does not pull the blanket back over her body. The leaving will be faster this way, kinder. Instead, he moves off a few feet, away from the road, away from the old mother, and gathers twigs and kindling into a pile and sets it ablaze with his torch. The frozen moisture in the ground will melt, make the digging easier.

Then, he takes his place beside the old woman, chanting the ancient words— words so old their meaning has been lost to the ages. His voice is barely a hum. It would not do to attract the soldier's attention. They do not understand that possessions belong with their owner, even in death. She will go to the darkening land with her bracelets and with ceremony; at least what ceremony he can give.

In the leaving, flesh melts from her face, until only hair and eyes sunk deep in her skull are all that seem to be left. The frozen vapor that marked her breath trails off.

The soft hoot of an owl sounds high in the hickory tree and tells him what he already knows. With a mighty throw, the old man sends a rock aloft and chases the harbinger of death away. The bird will not steal tonight's spirit.

He pushes the embers aside and tests the softened earth. The digging will not take long. She is shrunken and tiny and will not take up much room in the ground. His pot of red ochre is nearly empty, so he dips a thumb into the paint and runs a single line across her forehead. He removes the threadbare moccasins from her feet. It is not for her that he does this. It is so the living might not hear her walking around in the spirit world.

Though the woman is slight, he huffs with the exertion of lowering her body into the prepared crevice. His years are many and the old ones are leaving now. He worries that no one will be left to perform the ceremonies.

Her family has gone before her, lost to the coughing sickness, the fevers, the cold. He positions her so she will see their spirits when they come. Mounds of dirt sift down covering her face, her glittering bracelets, until nothing is left— nothing but the memory.

He pats the earth smooth. Living embers roll before the sweep of the shoulder bone until they are gathered on the mound. The fire spirit will discourage predators.

Out of respect for her memory, her name will not be spoken again.

Tired, his body groans aloud as he reaches for the government blanket and imagines her warmth still in the folds. He will give it to a young one. They are, after all, the people's future.

Overhead, the seven sisters sparkle like they did in the old land. It is a comfort. He sinks down and leans against the hickory tree, desperate for sleep. But the knowing comes again, prods him to his feet.

With a sigh, Death Keeper lifts his face to the night and tests the air, waiting to be shown the way.

Literary Short Story
Honorable Mention

Summer of '57
by
Leslie Daugherty

A few days before my eleventh birthday, Mother and I came to Fort Worth, Texas after her long overdue divorce from my father. Our new home, the Ripley Arnold Housing Project, took some adjustment on our part.

We'd moved just before the school term ended. At first I was glad school was out. Bored three weeks later because I had no friends to play with, I wandered my new territory. I went every day to the swings on the playground in front of the apartment units on Peach Street and waited for some kid to start a conversation. I was shy. Maybe tomorrow, I thought, and headed home for supper, crossing Peach Street. The hot asphalt cooked my bare feet.

Multi-colored vehicles lined the curb like a broken-back python. People didn't feel so destitute if they had an engine to gun and some way to escape the confines of that four block square of concrete hell on summer Saturdays. A couple of dads with their heads under the hood of an old car looked up as I went by, a skinny kid wearing an old dress that tied in a bow in the back.

The exhaust fumes atomized by the flow of traffic down Henderson Street gave off a motor-oily, metallic aroma, but couldn't cancel out the smell of food. The smells of pinto beans and fried potatoes hung in the atmosphere, layered between those of fried bologna and hamburger. The fragrances wafting from apartment doors beckoned like cartoon come-hither fingers, slithering invisibly under my nose. Starving, I followed their lead, hoping something appetizing waited for me at home.

As I rounded the corner to Cherry Street a blonde toddler ran toward me, landing stiffly on her short legs, curls bouncing. A tall, slim girl carrying a younger child ran to catch her. I accelerated my pace and intercepted the giggling tot to keep her from the street. The dark-haired girl couldn't move fast enough to catch her. I handed the child over.

"Thank you," she said. She scolded the pretty baby, "Don't you ever do that again," and lifted the runaway to her other hip. The mother's face between the two babies' golden heads formed a lovely triptych. Her skin, the color of cinnamon mixed with gold dust, glowed in the sunshine. She looked like a princess.

"She likes for me to chase her. It's a game we play in the house, but she plays it everywhere." The girl's lilting voice sounded bubbly and full of music.

"Where are you from?" I asked.

"Jamaica," she said. "We moved here a month ago. I'm Teresa. What's your name?"

"Lisa." I noticed her glass bracelet, the turquoise color vivid against her skin.

"Well, Lisa," she said, "Come visit us. We live up there in 408." She pointed to Bluff Street. "We don't know anyone here." I found her courtesy appealing.

"We don't either," I said. We talked a little, and said our goodbyes. I continued on my mission to find sustenance, passing the rows of red brick apartments.

People of all backgrounds lived in the subsidized housing in downtown Fort Worth back then. World War II vets in wheelchairs, people with other disabilities, widowed women, women and children who been abandoned.

Having previously lived in isolated country settings, I was unused to the activity and noise. Trucks, cars and ambulances rumbled and wailed down Henderson Street. Rude kids played in screeching bands. Moms in housedresses held hands to sun-squinted eyes to distinguish their young in the distance and shouted for them to come home. Above all that, a cacophony of stations blared from the open windows and doors. Fats Domino moaned lyrics. Older people turned their television sets so loud you could hear them outside. Ralph Kramden threatened Alice with lunar landings and Lucy got in messes punctuated by canned laughter.

We didn't have a T.V.

I propped a book on the napkin holder and read while I ate my sandwich.

* * * * *

The next morning, the prospect of another unfruitful day at the playground seemed a waste of time. I went to see Teresa, keeping my new acquaintance secret. She seemed glad to see me. She'd just fed the babies, who were covered in oatmeal. I volunteered to help bathe the children, feeling I had missed something not having siblings. After she knew me better, I entertained the kids while she cleaned the house or took a bath in peace. I felt very grown-up that she trusted me.

Her husband Eddie spent the weekdays looking for work. I met him one Saturday and he was not what I expected. The couple held a certain fascination for me.

Teresa had light chocolate silk skin. Eyes of amber, black lashes, and straight black brows etched a perfect, stunning face. Her long hair floated in a cloud around her face, the spiraling curls and fine texture betraying Spanish and African descent. Graceful, fluid movements, like a languid response to music no one else could hear, marked her passage as she tended her household.

I observed her patient, affectionate ways with her family. There was for me, of course, the attraction of the unusual. Holding those tawny, sloe-eyed babies was like holding a tiger cub on your lap. I combed tangles from their hair every day and watched the nimble art of Teresa's quick slender fingers braiding it.

She was my first experience with people of color.

There was a separate housing project on the other side of town for black people. Of course, the fact that Teresa was half-Spanish, and married to a white man put the housing authority in a quandary. They had to admit her to Ripley, but the mixed-race marriage put the couple in a situation for which there was little tolerance at that time.

There were repercussions I didn't understand. So what if Teresa was brown? Some of the people in the Projects were rude for no other reason. When someone slighted her, she lowered her beautiful eyes and said nothing. Her dignity transcended racism.

Blond hair and golden coloring gave Eddie a leonine appearance. He had crinkles around his startling blue eyes when he smiled. His thin, muscular body crackled with electricity and sinuous eloquence, like a downed power line. He was Lucifer fallen to earth, and provided an exquisite foil to Teresa's dark angelic appearance. Like Lucifer, he didn't suffer insults lightly.

Dissimilar as night from day, the young couple represented glamour and romance to me because they looked at each other sometimes with such affection and a kind of strange knowledge. Sometimes I felt embarrassed, as if I'd seen something I shouldn't have. I had never seen my parents look at each other like that.

Eddie, seeming to sense that I admired their devotion, enjoyed teasing me.

"Hey, good looking," he'd say, "You're gonna be fighting the boys off with a stick one of these days."

I could feel my face get red. But I loved to be around them. The warmth between them spilled over and gave me hope.

Mom first met Teresa one day when I stayed outdoors too late and she came to call me home. Teresa assured her I was no bother, but mother told me not to visit their house on the weekends when Eddie was home.

"People need time to themselves, you know," she said, implying that I might be overstaying my welcome. Mother said I was too old for my age and should play with other kids.

Later I began to wonder if she wasn't right. Maybe Eddie didn't really like me as much as I thought. After a few weeks I noticed a change. He stayed around the house during the week and grew very quiet. He laughed less and became abrupt with his wife. She took it in stride, explaining his behavior away. He got into an argument with a neighbor who had been his only friend. Though he was never rude to me, I was uncomfortable when he spoke sharply to Teresa. It made her unhappy and reminded me of my father. Sometimes I didn't stay long.

I wanted them to be the way they were before.

One morning Teresa and I sat on their front porch watching the babies play in the yard. Eddie stood in the street working on their old Chevy. Its carburetor stubbornly refused to surrender to his mechanical coercion. He made a few adjustments, got in and tried again to start the engine. When it coughed, but wouldn't turn over, he got out and slammed the door.

We watched him. Cigarette between his teeth, the smoke curled into his squinted eyes. He removed the breather with tapered fingers, blackened with grease. His shirtless shoulders glistened as he pulled out the filter and hit it flat on the sidewalk to clean it of loose dirt and bugs. James Brown moaned, "Please, please, please," from the radio sitting in the windowsill. Mentally I sang along, begging the carburetor to work. The slap, slap of the filter left dusty circles on the sidewalk. Eddie replaced it, but dropped the wing nut that held the breather in place. It landed underneath the car.

"Goddamn mother fucker!" Eddie barked.

A bloodrush sped up my heart, making my head feel full and my scalp tingly with fear, a familiar, unwelcome reaction, almost forgotten.

"Goddammit!" he muttered, eyes arcing blue voltage. "Son of a bitch." He kicked the tire. "I got places I need to be!"

Teresa gathered the kids. I followed her inside.

She turned to me. "You'd better go now," she said quietly. "Come back tomorrow."

"Okay," I said, looking for reassurance.

"It'll be fine. He's just in a bad mood."

I kissed both caramel-skinned babies, ruffled their curly ochre hair, and went home.

"Mom," I yelled when I opened the back door. "What's for supper?"

"It's on the stove," she yelled from upstairs. "I'll be down in a minute."

I filled a plate with fries, beans, and meatballs the size of walnuts.

Mom appeared with a head full of wire brush rollers and Pond's cold cream shining on her face, wearing her favorite old housedress.

"You're late," she said. "You were supposed to be home at six."

"I'm sorry. I was helping Teresa with the babies."

"You could do some things around here, you know." She cocked an eyebrow at me, and looked over the glasses whose earpieces she'd pushed through rollers pulled so tight her eyes slanted.

Handing me a glass of tea, she said, "Besides, you don't need to wear out their doormat."

"Teresa likes me to help her." I listed details of my valuable assistance, omitting the one about Eddie's show of temper.

* * * * *

At two in the morning, we were awakened by someone banging on our door. Mom opened it to find Teresa standing there, naked and shivering with humiliation.

"I didn't know where else to go," Teresa whispered, not looking up. I was the only friend she had.

Mom pulled her inside and covered her with a blanket from our couch. "Where are the kids?" she asked.

"They're with Eddie," Teresa said. Her lashes were wet and she looked stricken and gray in that strange way dark-skinned people have of going pale. "He slapped me and ripped off my nightgown. He pushed me out and wouldn't let me back in." She began to cry again and said, "He's drinking lately. He's never hit me before." She seemed dazed.

"He won't hurt the kids, will he?" Mom asked, furious.

"No. " Teresa said. "It's me he's mad at."

"Are you sure?"

"Oh, yes." Her face crumpled and she nodded. " I'm sure."

"Well, you're not going back there tonight." Mom said, not giving her a choice about the situation. "Things will look better in the morning." She sent me upstairs, put sheets on the couch for our visitor, and came up later. In those days a woman didn't call the police even if her husband was a closet gorilla. She wouldn't want anyone to know she was the kind of woman who got beaten. The police never did anything anyway and then she would have admitted to the whole world the shame of her husband not loving her. And for what?

There would be no convincing herself that he did when she saw pity or contempt in her neighbor's eyes.

Teresa cried quietly all night and went home the next morning in borrowed clothes.

"Stay away from there today." Mom said grimly before she left for work.

I worried, like always.

When I stepped up on the porch, I saw them in the kitchen through the gray haze of the screen door. Teresa sat in a chair facing me, wearing mom's purple housecoat. Eddie was on his knees in front of her, his arms around her waist. Muffled sobs shook him.

She rocked him, holding his head against her breast, her long fingers tangled in his thick, light hair.

"I'm sorry. I shouldn't have done it. I just get crazy sometimes."

"Shhh," she soothed him, looking me in the eyes.

She shook her head. I faded away from the doorway.

She explained later he'd said he regretted marrying her. He was sorry the next day. She wanted to believe it was liquor talking, and he didn't really feel that way.

Things went kind of back to normal, and I spent some time with them, against my mother's wishes. I circled the block so Mother wouldn't see me go in the direction of their house. She didn't think it was good for me to go there. I felt Teresa needed me.

Eddie knew my opinion would never be restored to its original luster. He couldn't look me in the eye at first, but soon returned to his old tactics, teasing and laughter. I went along with it for her sake, but he didn't win me over. I never liked him again. I knew the dangers of fooling myself.

A month later they were gone. Eddie had beaten Teresa and threatened her with a knife, putting her in the hospital. They were kicked out of the Projects before she was even dismissed by the doctor. Eddie had to scramble to find a place. Rules about drinking and weapons were strictly enforced in the government housing.

I never saw Teresa again.

I thought about the beautiful couple often in the days following their banishment, as they were when I first met them. I had basked in their glow. In spite of that early impression, I hoped for her sake that Teresa had taken the babies, left him, and gone home to Jamaica. But I doubted she would.

The princess loved the prince too much.

Sometimes there aren't any fairytale endings. Sometimes you simply have to find a way to live as happily ever after as you can.

I went back to the playground again and waited for some kid to start a conversation.

Literary Short Story Honorable Mention

Camping Out
by
Marilyn Gilbert Komechak

The woman awakened first and stepped from the small tent. The sky looked tortured in blood red furrows. Taking a deep breath she went back inside. The man slept with his chin tilted up, arms resting by his side as if he floated on water. She felt her brow tighten as she looked at him. Kneeling, she rummaged in a knapsack, pulled out a journal and began writing:

We wanted to live under this tree, along this river forever. But that was then, when we were one in everything we said or did. Now I speak a new language and he hears in the old one. Our harmony is gone and frustration has carved out the best part of my intellect and tossed it into the bushes—a wasted bone.

"What were you doing?" he asked, his eyes still closed.

"Looking at the sky."

He did not move or comment. She put the journal back into the bag and went out again. This time she walked all the way to the water's edge, sometimes slipping on the dew-wet grass. A sudden breeze crosshatched the water's ripples as she tentatively stepped backward, and then sat on the ground. Tiny eddies stroked the small stones at the bottom of the stream making them wobble in their places. A leaf swept past to disappear.

Out of the corner of her eye, she saw him come out of the tent dressed only in jeans. He put his hands on his hips, arched his back and began twisting his neck around. Then he picked his way down to where she sat on the grass. Still, she started when he touched her arm.

"Why are you sitting here?"

"I was thinking." She laughed as if uncertain, "Well, not thinking...only some words that came to mind."

"Like what?"

There was the intake of her own breath before she spoke. "That memories are foil-thin and rolling up at the edges." The sounds of her own voice struck her with its solemnity, as if she were reading aloud from a book.

A quizzical frown worked his features as he turned his gaze to look out across the water. Then out of the frown the question, "You got enough stuff for lunch?" She nodded. He headed back to the truck, slump-shouldered digging in his toes for traction. She felt the chilling draft of distance between them as it eroded their dream. He would never understand the person she had become. They were strangers now.

Then a yell, a roar. "Dammit!" He looked back at her. The look on his face as if she'd planted the sliver of glass he now dug out of his toe.

He hobbled to their sun-bleached, blue van parked near the tent. There was a scraping metallic groan as he lifted the hood. She looked up to see him, bent over the engine, tinkering inside the cavity. An oily smell wafted down. Minutes passed before he slammed the hood. She heard a moan as he squatted to look at the tires.

"I gotta go get some air 'n ice."

About noon he returned. They sat on opposite sides of the concrete picnic table. Stenciled across the top in orange letters was, "#116 property of Camp & Canoe Campground." She felt him looking at her.

"What did you do while I was gone?"

"Took a walk, wrote a little...nature notes. That sort of thing." She felt her brow tighten again as she said this.

"Let's eat," he instructed. She got out the leftover lunchmeat. He opened a bottle of Coke, pouring an equal amount into each paper cup. Then he went to get some ice from the chest. Scooping a handful, she watched as he dropped the ice into the already too full cups. With care, he wiped his wet hands on the sides of his jeans, a look of satisfaction on his face. The Coke overflowed making a puddle around each cup, staining the newspaper spread out on the table. "I'll wipe it up," she said.

"Don't bother. What's a little mess?"

She got up anyway and mopped up the spill. Moments passed. The only sound was their shallow breathing as they gazed in opposite directions.

Near sundown an old green Dodge truck, grinding and lurching, bounced into the space next to the van. A middle-aged woman they recognized as the owner of the campsite, and a young man with a camera, got out of the truck. The woman waved in friendly fashion as they came toward the couple seated at the table.

"Would y'all mind posin' for a picture? This man is from the Chamber of Commerce in town. He needs a picture for Star Travel Magazine of a couple enjoying the Tecumseh River."

"Sure...sure we'd be happy to," the man said as he got up to snatch a T-shirt hanging on the back of a near-by lawn chair. The campers sat with their backs to a radiant setting sun.

"Okay. You two sit close together. You, Mister, cozy-up there and put your arm around her shoulders an' look into her eyes."

* * * * *

Some months later she found the magazine on a rack at the drugstore. Two smiling people picnicked with a beautiful coral sunset dissolving behind them. Camp & Canoe Campgrounds were the only words on the page. A map and a phone number followed—no description, no story.

The woman, dressed for travel, stood motionless looking at the picture. Dying florescent light bulbs sent yellow flickers across the glossy page. She dug in her purse for a pen. Across the picture in flowing black script she wrote: *It was no picnic.*

She closed the magazine and put it back on the shelf. Nothing about the magazine's appearance suggested it had ever been opened.

Turning away, she picked up her suitcase and pushed open the screen door. As she walked to the bus stop, the sun slid below the horizon. The sidewalk echoed with her footsteps as purple shadows poured onto the broken, tilted concrete slabs, absorbing the sound, blurring the memories.

Flash Fiction ~ 1st Place

Baggage

by

Holly K. Snapp

She lies huddled on the kitchen tile, listening to the television channels cycling one after the other. Staccato bursts of commercials and canned laughter penetrate the haze, drawing her closer to the hurt.

Will's voice, insistent and rough, tries to wrench her up and into motion. "Get off your backside and bring me a sandwich!"

She ignores it. She can afford to now. What else can he take?

Breath whistles through her swollen throat and into lungs reluctantly expanding against ribs fractured by his work boots. The pain exists far off; he brought it to life, and it belongs to him. Each new inhalation surprises her, and she counts them, one, two, three...thirty eight. She is dimly amazed by her body's determination to spite him, and awed at its ability to persevere.

Something jagged cuts at the inside of her mouth—a tooth, lodged at an angle between the cheek and gum. It isn't worth the trouble to turn her head and spit it out. Why bother, with time so short? She's debated with herself long enough, and finally she will go, embark on a voyage, sail off to the land of Someplace Else. Who would have foreseen that he would be the one to give her the ticket?

First she will gather her belongings, things she can't bear to go without. Her suitcase, a wedding gift never once used, appears, and as she gazes at it the misery vanishes from her arms, her legs, her back and ribs. Even the broken tooth stops hurting.

Grateful, she rises and begins to pack.

She won't leave without the taste of the air after summer's last big storm, the one that broke the heat wave holding them captive in its airless heart for so many weeks. She also needs the smell of fresh coffee and the gurgling sigh of the pot when it brews.

She throws in the sensation of her toes digging into dewy morning grass, the decadent flavor of rich French chocolate, and the flutter of her heart when, as a little girl, she soared high, so high, almost to the clouds, on her backyard swing. The music of her mother's voice must come too, and she puts it next to the scent of lilacs and the joy of sliding between sheets dried in the sun.

Last, but not least, she tucks in the shy feathery brush of his lips against hers, back when she still inspired tenderness in him.

She closes the bag, snaps its latches, and buckles the straps. She lifts it, marveling at the weightlessness...and turns to go.

Harry the Horse
by
Art Youmans

"Are you Harry the Horse?"

"Yeah, that's me."

The pug-faced guy points to a limousine. "The boss wants to see you!"

One day, I knew it would come to this. Some people have perfect pitch and become famous singers; others have coordinated muscles and develop into great athletes. It's genetic. With me, I'm a genius at the racetrack.

The pug opens the rear door of the limousine. A small man in the backseat smiles and extends his hand. "Harry the Horse. Glad to finally *meetcha.*" He signals the driver out of the car with a wave of his fingers. I stare as the driver and pug lean against a telephone booth across the street.

"Do ya know who I am?" he asks in a soft voice.

"Yes. You run the St. Louis mob."

"Do ya know why we're meeting?"

"I'm not sure."

"Take a guess, Harry."

I look out the window and see two others have joined the pug and driver. "Well, I've had a bit of luck lately on the ponies," I say.

"Hell," he interrupts, "your winning bets bankrupted our Oklahoma bookies and closed down Remington Park. Horse racing's nearly died in Oklahoma because of you!"

I wipe the sweat from my forehead and look him in the eye. "Mr. Costello…"

"Call me Frank."

"Okay, Frank. I've been called 'Harry the Horse' all my life. Since I was a kid I could tell which racehorse would win at any track. It was a gift. When other kids were reading books, I was studying the *Racing Form.*"

"How come you never lose?"

"Oh, I lose, sometimes. I lost on Violinist and Silver Bullet in '96."

"Hell, they both lost in photo finishes. You ain't lost since!"

" I seem to know what horse will win."

"Harry. I'd like you to stop betting on the ponies and come work for me."

"I can't do that, Frank. Betting is the only thing in life I'm good at. It's in my genes."

Frank pushes a button and the trunk opens. He signals for me to get out. We walk to the back of the limousine and stare into the trunk.

"*Whatcha* see?" he asks.

"A pair of shoes."

"Get 'em!"

I try to lift them. "They weigh a ton," I said. "What are they made of? Concrete?"

Frank smiles. "How'd you guess? They're size 11D."

"That's my size," I say. "What a coincidence."

"It ain't no coincidence."

A light bulb goes on in my head. I look him in the eye and say, "Frank, you have a gift of persuasion. I'd be happy to work for you."

"Do you have any questions?"

"Yeah, just one. What are you gonna do with those concrete shoes?"

He grins. "We'll keep 'em handy in case you ever change your mind."

I gulp. "It's in my genes, Frank. Once I make my mind up, I never change it."

And I never did.

Short Story ~Young Adult~ 1st Place

Smashdown
by
Joan Minor

The roar of the departing Coweta school bus drowns out my horrified 'Eeek' as I notice the telephone pole. What's got me so upset? My mom's face stares down at me from the pole. Well, actually Mom isn't hanging up there. Her picture is though.

I haven't seen Mom since the day last fall when she grabbed the short, fireplug-shaped lady by her blonde pony tail and slammed her to the floor. As if that wasn't enough to make me scrunch down and hide, Mom head-butted the tattooed woman who rushed to help her fallen friend.

If I close my eyes, the scene rewinds in my head. A huge grin splits Mom's face as she spots me in the screaming crowd. She waves and squeals, "Olivia, baby! I didn't know you wuz here."

The only reason I, Olivia Thomas, 15-year-old daughter of Torrie Thomas, didn't instantly die of shame? Mom split soon after that, leaving me and Dad alone. He got so depressed he said we had to get away, move to a new town. A new state. So we moved from Kansas to Coweta, Oklahoma—where I bump elbows with dozens of potential friends at high school every day.

Mom's a dark secret in my new life.

I had hoped she'd remain that way. But to my horror, the poster I just spotted says Torrie will soon burst upon Coweta—with dire consequences for me:

Wanna Wrestle?
U.S. Smashdown Visits Coweta Arena, Nov. 1
Starring Torrie Thomas!

"Why didn't dad tell me?" I mutter. Now everyone will discover Mom's not an archeologist living in Italy.

My friend Mike McCoy knows the truth, but he's sworn to secrecy. Mike's chatter pulls me back into the moment because I momentarily spaced out after I re-read the words *Wanna Wrestle*. The color picture of Torrie posing in a scarlet boob tube and gold satin hip huggers doesn't help my wooziness either.

I blink to clear my blurred vision. Overhead, teal-edged clouds dance across Oklahoma's spring sky. Scissortails swoop and hopscotch back and forth through the trees. I suck in air to steady my nerves. The wind throws a dust devil at me. Instead of relaxing, I choke on a mouthful of dirt. Tears gush down my cheeks and I strangle and gag.

16

Mike pounds me on the back. "Whoa...you okay?"

"Yeah, but I don't think I can deal with Torrie—those wrestling matches are so fake, so tacky." I groan. "Mom's behavior is deeply despicable and totally trashy and awfully appalling and increasingly insensitive..."

Mike slaps his hands over his ears. "Stop! Please." He shakes his head. "I admire your awesome vocabulary, but it could be worse."

"How?" I squawk.

"She could be ugly."

"Oooh, Mike, sometimes you are so shamefully shallow."

"She's hot! Gorgeous. Plus, she hasn't been laid..." Mike glances at me. A blush stains his cheeks. "I mean, she hasn't been pinned on the mat by an opponent in nine matches." His purple cowlick bounces as the wind ripples through his hair.

I ignore Mike's immature and totally gross comments, but see what I mean? No other girl in school worries about people commenting on their mother being laid.

"Females! Smashdown wrestling." Mike jumps in a circle and lands in front of me. "Wowza! Your mom's the queen of Smashdown—she'll tear Coweta contenders apart." Sunlight sparkles on the gold rings that pierce his eyebrows and ears.

If I didn't truly appreciate Mike's friendship, I'd punch him in the nose.

Eeiyew, I sound like Mom. Is there a smashdown gene? Am I about to burst out of what Dad calls my joyless gray slump and attack a friend?

"I can't believe this. All my beautiful plans...my budding friendships... everyone at school will laugh at me if they discover my mother is a one-woman, muscle-bound demolition crew instead of an archeologist. Why didn't Dad tell me she was coming?"

"Why did you tell everyone she lived in Italy?"

"I don't know—lots of reasons. Italy's so terra-cotta, so *la dolce vita*—you know, the sweet life. Also, maybe it's because I love Clint Eastwood's old spaghetti westerns?" I shrug. "The Leaning Tower of Pizza?"

"Pisa, doofus."

"To be honest, I said she lived in Italy because I wanted her to be a continent away, even if it was in my dreams."

Mike's eyes narrow. "Better cool off a minute—your complexion's gone all splotchy red." He peers closely at my face. "Your cheek's dotted with yellow patches."

I feel my forehead with my left hand. Hmm, feverish. "Yikes!" I point in horror. "My brain must be bleeding—everything's gone red. Look at that tree on the corner."

Mike turns and stares. He studies the tree that's vibrating with an intense rosy glow. "That's a redbud."

"A what?"

"A redbud tree—Oklahoma's state tree."

"Oh."

"Mistletoe's our state flower."

"A fungus?"

His eyes widen in shock. "Wow, you surprise me, most girls just think of kissing under the mistletoe."

"Don't say that word; it makes me nauseous—just like Torrie and her wrestling match. What am I going to do?" Without thinking, I yank the cardboard down and rip it into confetti.

"Olivia…" Mike grabs my wrist.

I jerk away and stare at the shredded paper scattered at my feet. Suddenly my brain cells crackle. I know how to crush her Smashdown plans. "I'll tear down all the posters. Destroy her publicity. No one will buy any tickets. The match will be canceled."

"Stop," Mike yells as I race toward the next pole. "You'll get arrested."

I screech to a halt. Sharp gravel bits sting my shins. "Okay, we can do it after dark—when no one's looking." My bangs swirl in a brown curtain across my face. I poke them behind my ear.

"Whoa, stay cool. What do you mean we?" Mike asks.

Our eyes meet—his still merry and blue, mine brown and probably desperate. "You have to help me get rid of them. It's total humiliation for me if she crashes into town."

Mike frowns. "I'm already in trouble. Can't chance it." He saunters across his family's yard of rough grass sprinkled with bright dandelions and clumps of purple henbit. Mike's skinny arms flap as he jumps onto his home's sagging front porch.

"Mike," I plead, "I thought you'd borrow your brother's car and drive me…" A *click* signals a closed door that shuts me out. "*Ciao*," I whisper.

Okay, so I'm alone. Afoot. Well, this won't stop me. I'll have to be careful though. Coweta's main street isn't a sedate, small-town boulevard. It's more of a fast-moving highway, but there won't be much traffic late at night. I'll breeze through the job.

My plans proceed. After supper I tell Dad I have homework and zip to my room. I hop into bed, dressed for my escapade in black T-shirt and jeans. I pull my purple comforter around my neck to hide my special-forces type apparel and yell, "Good night."

I'm so juiced I can't stay under the covers very long. I grab my red math book and figure a few number puzzles. Next, I snatch a blue English textbook, doodle through a host of mysterious verb conjugations. I file that piece of work away.

Moving on, I check what's left at the bottom of the homework pile. Hmm, why do teachers assign so many themes? Take this one for example, a "Steps to Future Success" paper due next week in Family Living.

Minutes tick past. I keep thinking about *my* so-called family living. Torrie wasn't content to abandon me and Dad. Now she's out to destroy our new life in Coweta.

Well, I won't let her.

Midnight finally arrives. I inch the window open and peer around. The night is clear and warm. A hush blankets our neighborhood. The blue-white streetlights radiate a glow that will illuminate my work. I sling a leg over the sill, clamber out, and race through the night to prevent a catastrophic blow to my reputation.

Several hours later I feel lower than a car squatting on four flat tires. Like totally deflated. I got caught, though I'm not actually behind bars. I slouch on a bench at the police station. A nosy clerk at Foley's Gas and Big Gulp convenience store saw me ripping down posters and alerted the law. Naturally, Dad was contacted.

Uh oh, a door swooshes. Dad's voice. The heavy thump of footsteps approaches. Goose bumps cascade over me as I wonder what he's going to say. Even worse, what will he do?

* * * * *

The next day, I find out. What a cliché! How trite. Dad grounds me. Plus, though it doesn't make sense, he keeps me home from school. He's ashamed. He can't control his own daughter.

I shout, "You ought to be ashamed of Torrie! Why didn't you control your wife when she ran off to be a wrestler? Then maybe I wouldn't have been driven to..." I can't finish.

Naturally Dad finishes for me. "Sneak out in the middle of the night? Break the law?" He roars, "Abuse my trust?!" As he paces, his shoulders slump. Bald head shines. Plaid shirt bulges over his tummy. Khakis rumple and trip him with each stumble-bumble step. For a moment my heart aches for him.

"Just wait...," he whimpers, "until your mother gets here."

Oooh, this is below the belt. He called Torrie. That's why he kept me home from school.

* * * * *

Torrie arrives the next day, one day late—which isn't surprising–and she charges in without knocking. Her ego knows no bounds. She thinks she owns the place and still has the right to have her say about me.

"Olivia, what wuz you thinking?" She shakes her head. Her tawny blonde hair cascades onto her shoulders. Blueberry-bright eyes sparkle with, of all things, admiration. "What spunk—I might sign you as my new tag-team partner." She chuckles. The sound is hoarse and raspy. Torrie smokes. The woman is a walking bad habit.

Then her true nature shows. Torrie's eyes narrow to slits. "My career is too important to be jerked down here for nothin'. We'll put you in a home for delinquents if you don't straighten up."

Dad collapses. Holds his head.

What a wimp. A sigh escapes me. I study my parents. Torrie torrid in a red satin jumpsuit; Dad rumpled in dismay and defeat. Two people I don't really know. I've never had a meaningful conversation with either of them.

What do they have to do with me?

Absolutely nothing? Absolutely everything?

I study these people who created me and realize—they aren't me. I don't have

19

to be ashamed of what they do, though it will be hard not to wince at Torrie's career path. I just have to make sure I don't do things to shame myself—like lying and breaking rules and sneaking around.

I'm the only person who can humiliate me.

I leave the room. My parents don't notice. Torrie's gravel voice grinds away at Dad. He comatoses into a private world.

I shut my bedroom door and shiver as I cross the room to lower the wide-open window. A chilly spring rain whispers against the glass. I flick on a lamp. Its golden glow warms the shadows. It's a cozy little bedroom and I'm thankful I've got a place that makes me feel safe. Even though Dad and I have only lived in this house since last fall, peace and security reign in my room because of familiar belongings that haven't changed.

But I still jerk every time I hear Torrie's voice yelling at Dad.

I surprise myself with the thought that leaps into my gray matter—maybe school work will settle my nerves. The Family Living workbook teeters on a pyramid of dirty socks, my blue and white track uniform, a crushed Cheeto's bag, an empty rumpled, crumpled Twinkie box, and about twenty CDs and DVDs.

Thoughts buzz. The Family Living textbook says: *Success isn't avoiding hurt; it's learning to deal with it.*

I open the workbook, scrap the first few paragraphs of the homework paper, and the words flow:

Be a Smashing Success!
By Olivia Thomas

"Draft 1"
One who is optimistic and capable of confronting failure or adversity with a smile and positive attitude, is the one who succeeds.

Yes, I know, that's copied almost verbatim from the textbook. I'll change it later. I continue writing...

When my mother Torrie Thomas started on the road to success, she didn't realize it would take her on a strange journey that included failure at an Italian archeological dig to Queen of Smashdown Wrestling.

Okay. I know, I know. I cannot continue to lie about Torrie. But how am I going to break it to my friends at school that my mother is a wrestler.

"Draft 2"
When my mother launched her wrestling career...

Whoa, should I spit out the truth about Torrie like this? No, I can't. But what am I going to do? How do I fix this mess so I won't be afraid?

"Draft 3"

Sometimes it's hard to admit the truth when you've done something stupid. I did that. I pretended to be something I wasn't so I'd look like a success. But now I realize if the first step you take toward success is based on a lie, then you've built yourself a pretty wobbly launching pad.

I flop back on the bed—totally exhausted. Writing is tough. But hard work is supposed to build character, and I'll need plenty of that when I get up to read this paper in class. Ooh, the thought hits me like a shot of adrenalin straight to the heart—standing in front of the class...saying my thoughts out loud. Life *is* full of scary things—no wonder you build it step by step.

The Kelvinator Man
by
Leslie Daugherty

A few days ago I had lunch with a girlfriend. Divorced twice, she vented steam about her most recent dating disappointment while I perused the menu and decided on a Caesar salad. She dined on potato skins along with some choice cuts of her last boyfriend, roasted over the coals and peppered with spicy verbs. She's lost faith in men and exudes despair at the prospect of growing old alone. This gal is statuesque and beautiful, but depression has made her negative, which as we all know, is simply death to male attraction.

"The bloom is off the rose," she wailed.

I told her, "Bobbie Sue,"—that's her name. "Bobbie Sue," I said, "You gotta have confidence. You're still a fine flower of southern womanhood." I extolled her virtues all through dessert, trying to encourage her.

We went to my house after lunch. I retrieved two Cokes from the fridge in the garage on the way into the kitchen.

"Have you still got that old thing?" she asked. It was an idle reference to the ancient Kelvinator. Everybody has a second car. I have a second refrigerator. It's roughly the same age as my marriage contract, and I wax sentimental about it, much as any car aficionado would about a '57 Chevy.

"Yep," I swigged my icy drink. "They don't build 'em like that anymore." It works wonderfully and holds the Thanksgiving dinner overflow. The aging, rounded contours lend it a certain hulking charm and magnitude. In a strong wind, I fancy that it keeps the house from blowing away.

We retired to the couch in the den, kicked off our shoes, and picked up the frayed threads of our conversation. Bobbie Sue says I'm out of touch with the reality of relationships today because I've been married to my first husband for thirty-seven years and can't possibly comprehend the shortage of viable males. I argue that though it's undeniable she has dated a few amphibians, her prince is still out there.

She counters my every reassurance about her love life with more "buts" than a nude beach. "But, Mary Beth, she complains, "All the good ones are taken."

I don't think that's necessarily so, I say.

"But they all want younger women," she says.

I remind her of men we know who date women their age.

"But they're all so dull," she whines.

So the afternoon went. By two o'clock I was almost wondering what I saw in her myself. However, I still felt it was my duty to offer solace in her time of tribulation. I decided to tell her about my cousin Lou Ann who married more often than Liz Taylor yet found true love in the end.

Lou Ann has what we used to call "it." She is well liked by both men and women, but of course it's the men we're interested in here. Now, I don't know what indefinable combination of qualities "it" is. It is not personality. Lots of us have that. It's not sex appeal. It's not beauty. Even at seventy, plain as a mud fence, and so bow-legged she couldn't hem up a pig in a ditch, people of both genders and all ages continue to find my cousin charming.

Lou Ann just wed for the eighth time, this time to her high school sweetheart, Joe Bob. The only reason she didn't marry him in the first place is her family had more money than the Vatican and Bank of America and they thought Lou Ann could do better. They broke her and Joe Bob up and took her to Europe for a long vacation, and do you know what? By the time she got back Joe Bob had gone and married some little ole blonde floozie.

So Lou Ann proceeded to marry, and by golly she was good at it. These men were no slouches either. One was an airline pilot, one a diplomat in Belgium, one an engineer, one a lawyer, one a doctor, and one an artist of some reputation in Maine. One had an "awl bidness" over in Odessa. I might have lost one in the crowd. I don't know what Joe Bob does but he owns a small town here in Texas.

Lou Ann's first marriage lasted several years, but the rest got progressively shorter in duration. I reckon her ability to put up with aggravation dwindled in direct proportion to her increasing age.

Lou Ann says she envies the lasting quality of my marriage but bless her heart, I can tell she secretly thinks I could have done better if I'd just kept trying. I can't imagine being married to eight strangers, having to learn their ways and teach them mine. I mean, maybe I am behind the times because I've been married so long, but I always say if it ain't broke, don't work on it.

My marriage is comparable to our old Kelvinator out in the garage. You can count on it. It's outlasted the three or four "new and improved" ones I've had in my kitchen. It's nicked and scratched from kicking the door shut, but it still preserves important things and sustains its owners. Humming right along, it does its job. It doesn't have to have its paint or ego stroked. It knows it's appreciated. My husband is like that, too.

The late models look good, but about all you can count on them for is to make ice out of themselves. The Kelvinator has been faithful in service for lo, these many years, and I just can't bring myself to discard it. That would be like stabbing it right in the compressor. Besides, most of the year-end closeouts only have a one-year warranty. I'd hate to bust up a long-term relationship for that.

You know, Lou Ann had her share of unhappiness and I'm glad she and Joe Bob got together. But honestly, I have to wonder if she couldn't have been just as content a long time ago. I attribute some of Lou Ann's problems to the fact that her family was so "upwardly mobile." My aunt and uncle spoiled their kids rotten. But I think it was a disadvantage, having everything so young.

Lou Ann likes things to be new all the time—new men, new cars, new houses, new furniture, and new clothes. She likes things and, I suspect, husbands to be perfect.

My family, on the other hand, was horizontally mobile. I hate trailer houses.

I like permanence. I like old people, old houses, old cars, antiques and anything that has a history. I don't mind if my furniture has a scratch with a story behind it or my husband watches too much football.

I adore Lou Ann, though. I'm no more impervious to her charm than anyone else. She's loads of fun and we get along like a house afire when we're together. I really hope Joe Bob turns out to be as permanent a fixture in her life as my old fridge and my husband are in mine.

Well, back to Bobbie Sue. I told her all about how Lou Ann has had more men than Julia Roberts and Brittany Spears put together. Not just had 'em either, honey. They married her. Men get committed to Lou Ann faster than psychopaths to the nuthouse. She gets them sewed up, signed on the dotted line, and delivered to the altar. They all seem happy as pigs in the sunshine right up until her lawyer serves the papers.

But you know, I think I understand what happens to all of Lou Ann's Holy Unions. After a while the gloss wears off. Lou Ann starts noticing all their flaws. Pretty soon she can't see anything *but* shortcomings. The outcome is predictable. She gets restless, orders new appliances, and redecorates a perfectly good house. I don't know if she's trying to satisfy her discontent, forestall the inevitable, or just make sure the house is in top shape when she gets it in the property settlement. My cousin always leaves a marriage in better shape than it found her.

Anyhow, Lou Ann is living proof that there are plenty of men out there to marry. I mean, all by herself, she found eight of them.

I thought all that was pretty inspiring, but after I finished my tale Bobbie Sue still insisted on her mulligrubbing and *refused* to be lifted from the hangdog doldrums by the shining example of Lou Ann's sheer voluminousity of husbands.

Of all the nerve!

"Bobbie Sue," I snapped, "Grow up and smell the freon, honey! If you ever run across a good Kelvinator man, even if he has a few dents, you load that sucker up and take him home!"

Short Story ~ Science Fiction
First Place
Ride
by
Carmen Jasso

Bleary-eyed, soaked and hungry, Solomon was about to give up hope of getting out of the cool night's deluge. The idling car parked on the shoulder of the road was the first vehicle in three hours to come along the deserted stretch of highway.

His lanky body shivered. He tightened the belt on his trench coat, then began his walk to the car. A grin eased across his face as he realized it held only one person. *Bingo. Maybe my luck is changing.* Exhausted from the wait, but confident another trusting fool would soon be his next conquest, he found the strength to leap into a run to cover the remaining distance.

Solomon slid to a stop, jerked open the door and climbed in. He fastened his seatbelt before turning his attention to the driver. He pressed his lips tightly together to squelch the joyous laughter bursting within at the sight before him. *Perfect.*

The driver, a plus size woman, had been poured into her black mini skirt, sheer blouse and fishnets. Her shortly-cropped, burgundy hair stood at odd angles and an eclectic mix of costume jewelry adorned her plump neck and arms. A yellow and blue tattoo of an ankh decorated the back of her right hand. Black-lined, cherry-red lips smiled at him.

"Hi. I'm Novena. Almost didn't see you through all the damn rain." She snapped her bubble gum.

Cheap and trashy. He wiped water from his eyes. "Thanks for stopping. I thought I'd have to start swimming soon." He held out his callous hand. "I'm Solomon."

She shook his offered hand. Novena placed the car in gear and pulled back onto the road. She said, "I don't usually stop for hitchhikers, but you looked like a drowned cat, no offense. To be honest, I could use the company. Where you heading?"

"Wichita." His eyes surveyed the car's worn interior. Empty chip bags, candy and assorted junk food wrappers littered the seats and floorboards. A werewolf bobble doll affixed to the cracked dash grinned at him. From the rearview mirror, a fuzzy bat swung in lazy circles as though in flight. *Another freak. The world should thank me for getting rid of one more of its parasites.*

Novena blew and popped a large, pink bubble. "Great, I'm driving through it." She gave him a sly smile and asked, "Got a girlfriend waiting on you in Wichita?"

"Several." Visions of contorted faces brought a smile to his face. "You ever been there?"

"Sure. I've a lot of fond memories of Wichita. I learned to hunt there."

"A hunter. I'm one myself." He continued to look about the car. *Time to change the subject.* "What brings you driving through the heartland?"

"I'm traveling to surprise friends. I've been on the road for ten hours and still have about two more. I ran out of things to do to keep awake hours ago." Aware he was taking in his surroundings, she added, "Excuse the mess. You're welcome to any of the munchies back there."

"Thanks." Solomon twisted to face the rear seat and lifted a bag. *This is going to be so easy. Nice and fat just as I like them. They can't run fast enough to get away but they're quick enough to give me a good chase.*

Once again seated forward, he rummaged through the sack. "Novena. That's an interesting name."

She laughed. "Yeah, it's a Catholic devotion of prayers on nine consecutive days for a special purpose. My parents idea of a joke."

"I like it. Why is it a joke?"

"You'd have to know my parents. They have a strange sense of humor. My brothers and I all have unique names. My brothers are Angelus, Cleric and Parish."

After selecting a bag of strawberry licorice, he pulled out a string of the red candy. "And very religious names."

She snapped her gum. "My family's never been religious. That's why our names are so funny."

Solomon's favorite memory of his own father flittered through his mind; his first hunt. Remembering the thrill of that kill always brightened his day. *Dad never knew what hit him.*

He asked, "When was the last time you saw your folks?"

"Last month in Oklahoma City. We got together, had a few drinks and ate a cow."

"Don't you mean had a barbeque?"

"Yeah. That's what I meant." She popped another bubble.

He clenched his jaws. *That stupid gum is just another reason.* He took a deep breath and asked, "So, your friends don't know you're coming for a visit?"

"Nope. I should have called but I wanted to see their faces when I unexpectedly showed up on their doorstep." Out of the corner of her eye, she watched him toy with the licorice.

"What were you doing to keep awake?" He tied a single knot on the string then began another.

"Sang with the radio. Made a shopping list. Had a few bites of food. Dreamed about an exotic vacation. The usual stuff people do when bored on a long trip." Her eyes flickered to his hands playing with the candy. "And chewing gum. Lots and lots of it. Want a piece?" She reached for the ashtray to retrieve a package.

"No." He gritted his teeth. "Thanks, but I don't like the stuff."

Novena shrugged and returned her attention to the rain slick road.

26

Solomon asked, "You mind if I turn on the radio?"

"Go ahead, but I don't think we can get a decent station way out here. At least there hasn't been one since leaving Joplin."

He shoved the licorice into his mouth before switching on and tuning the radio. Finding nothing but static, he clicked it off. *No music for the entertainment.*

"You're right. No stations. How about we play a game?"

Novena cracked her gum. "Oh. Well...well, I'm not really good at games."

"You don't know what kind it is." Solomon ripped several more pieces of the candy from the bag then twisted the strands around his index fingers.

"True." She flexed her hands on the steering wheel. "Look. I don't mean to be a pain, but would you please eat those."

His eyes lowered to the candy then back up to her face. "Sure. What's the big deal?" He popped the pieces into his mouth.

"Sorry. It's a pet peeve of mine. My parents drilled into my brothers and me to never play with our food. I can't seem to break myself from it."

"No problem. Never play with your food? Interesting." Solomon tore another piece. "As I was saying, let's play a game to pass the time. How about trivia?" He sifted through the contents of another plastic grocery sack and a wicked smile slashed across his face. *This will drive her nuts.*

"I love animal cookies." He withdrew two horses out of the box and galloped them across the dash.

"Like I said I'm not good at games. Really I'm not." She blew another bubble. "Are you going to eat those?"

"Sure. Sorry. I forgot. It annoys you." He continued to knock together the heads of the cookie horses.

Exasperated, she blew out a breath. "Okay. Okay. What game?"

He ate the cookies then picked out two more, tossed them into the air and caught them with his mouth. As he munched, he mumbled, "How about the alphabet game?"

Novena glanced at him. "I've never heard of the alphabet game. How's it played?"

She gasped as the car suddenly lurched into the other lane. Novena tightened her grip and fought the steering wheel. Once back in control, she edged the vehicle onto the road's shoulder and maneuvered it to a stop.

Her voice trembled. "Great. Just great. We blew a tire." She switched off the ignition, retrieved the keys and threw open the door. "I've got a spare. Leave your door open. It's so dark out here, we need all the light possible."

As Novena pulled herself from her seat, Solomon's eyes gleamed. The hunt had just started without warning. His heart began to race; the need for release was stirring and building. He could not deny his passion any longer. *I couldn't have picked a better place. How the heck did I get this lucky?* Solomon hurried to meet her at the rear of the car. He said, "At least the rain stopped." He eyed their surroundings and licked his lips. "Sure is deserted. Someone could get lost and never be found."

Novena spit her gum out. "Yeah." She leaned into the trunk, lifted a box containing several bottles of red wine and placed it on the wet ground.

Solomon quickly checked both ways down the highway. He reached into the pocket of his jeans and retrieved a long, red, satin ribbon with a thin wire that ran inside its entire length. He carefully wrapped its ends around each of his hands. Let the game begin.

Novena removed a beaten suitcase, shifted items within the trunk and finally uncovered the spare tire. "Hope it's not flat. I haven't checked it in months." She turned to him and her eyes widened at the taut ribbon stretched between his clenched fists. "What the hell?" She backed a step and came up hard against the car.

Solomon advanced toward her. "You don't deserve to live. You're unclean, one of the diseased." He could not hide the disgust in his voice. "I've made a game of doing the necessary work." He stepped closer. "And guess what? You're the next player."

She nervously swallowed. "But why? I stopped to help you." Behind her back, she felt around in the trunk.

He sneered. "What kind of a woman stops and picks up a total stranger? Look how you're dressed. You're a whore!"

Novena edged toward the side of the car.

"Don't even think about it. Now, let's go over the rules." Solomon's hollow laugh rang through the quiet night. "Actually there aren't any rules. You run. I chase. I kill you. So why don't you start running so we can begin?"

Her lips slowly parted into a smile.

"What are you smiling at?" The sound of fluttering wings and a slight movement in the corner of his eye caused him to whirl around.

Into the small ring of pale illumination cast by the car's interior light, three large men, dressed in black, appeared to physically separate from the darkness and move as one to stand before Solomon.

He jumped at Novena's soft voice.

"Meet my brothers."

Goosebumps broke over both of Solomon's arms and a shiver crawled up his spine. He could not take his eyes off the intimidating men.

Novena repeated his words. "You don't deserve to live. You're unclean, one of the diseased." She placed a cool hand on his shoulder. "But unlike you, it's not a game. I just kill you."

He turned his head in her direction and froze.

Black skeletal appendages slowly grew from Novena's back. She arched her spine to unfurl and spread the new limbs wide to reveal leathery bat wings. Her fangs gleamed in the faint glow of the trunk's single light bulb.

What's going on? This isn't real! Fear as he had never known seized him. The faces of his previous prey flashed through his mind; their pleading eyes filled with fear and anguish. *Was this what they felt?* The very things he craved to see in their eyes now overwhelmed him. The exhilaration of the hunt was gone. For the first time in his miserable and warped existence, Solomon lost control of his bladder. As the wetness spread across his crotch and down his legs, tears spurted from his terror-filled eyes.

Solomon made to move. From one blink to the next, Novena stood beside him. She shoved him and he sprawled face down into a puddle of mud. The ribbon flew from his hands. She grasped his right arm, flipped him onto his back and straddled his struggling body.

With the wind knocked out of him and Novena seated across his abdomen, Solomon coughed and gulped in air. He thrashed about until she pinned his arms to the ground. His heart pounded furiously. *How can this be happening? I deserve to live! These things aren't even human! I'm the hunter, not prey!*

Silhouetted in the emerging full moon's fleeting glow, her brothers stood behind her with their huge wings flapping and beating the air around them. Their lips pulled back into ghastly snarls, emphasizing their fangs.

Novena leaned over, kissed his ear and whispered, "The only difference is...we don't play with our food."

As her teeth sank into his neck and his world began to fade, Solomon watched her brothers change the bullet-pierced tire, preparing for Novena's next road trip and her next ride.

Short Story ~ Mystery/Suspense ~ First Place

Out of Time
by
Valerie Gawthrop

I feel the ticking of the clock is the heartbeat of the home—but not tonight. The ticking...I covered my eyes, staring blankly at my collection.

Fifties starburst clocks, Black Forest cuckooes and vintage Schoolhouses, among others, covered every inch of wall space. Due to my constant vigilance each one read exactly 11:59. I held my breath. Time froze for an instant then moved along with scores of hour and minute hands.

Midnight. The chiming of the clocks drove all thought and reason from me. But not even the familiar din could wipe away the sight of the broken body.

I'd seen bodies before. I'd fought two wars, afterall. Still, there was something about the body on the floor...He was a stranger. Wasn't he? I referenced the photos on the fireplace mantle.

She wore a sheer, white dress over a satin slip. Lizzy? Was that her name? She was so young. She was giving a young man a pocket watch, a wedding present, the start of a collection. There were bushels of sunflowers on the church steps, wheat fields waving in the background...The watch ticking in perfect time to a perfect world...But the world doesn't stay perfect, does it?

I dug in my pocket, fingered the golden disk. Once, I'd loved the ticking of time. When I shared it with Lizzy...When I'd known the day of the week. Before unfeeling strangers began poking, prodding me, insisting that I take more medication.

I squinted at the body. A thief probably, someone who'd invaded my home to steal by clocks...They were always trying to steal from me. They'd stolen Lizzy, hadn't they?

My cane was sticky with blood. How did that get there? I used it to turn him over. Just enough to see his face...Familiar. I gripped the slick, bloody walking stick tighter. It was important to remember. Once again I searched the photographs on the mantle.

I saw it. The likeness of a man, or rather, a boy dressed in a graduation gown, his arm around Lizzy. She appeared older than in her wedding picture, still beautiful. She looked so proud.

I squinted, peered at the body. Our son? What was he doing here? There were papers scattered all about him. They looked like legal documents, the kind they're always trying to get me to sign. Papers meant to imprison me in the dementia

30

cell of an assisted care facility. I'd have to give up my clocks. Impossible. The ticking...The heartbeat...

I wiped blood off my hands, pulled the watch out of my pocket, flipping it open. It wasn't easy with my fingers all gnarled and bent. So much time had passed. I stared at the clocks on the wall. The watch was sixty-two seconds slow. I'd have to reset it as soon as I could trust my hands. For now, they trembled as I slipped the watch back into my pocket.

Short Story ~ Mystery/Suspense
Honorable Mention

American Visitor Disappears in Yorkshire
by
Margaret Hope

Testimony of Norah Barnacle, Housekeeper

T he renter at Clifford Grange introduced herself to me as Molly Lightfoot; she asked me to call her Molly. She'd come from Oklahoma—one of those academic people who'd been visiting Haworth for a donkey's years. She was little more than forty, surely, and you'd need the eye of a hawk to see the gray in her straight black hair. She wasn't always smiling as Americans do, saying, *So happy to be in jolly olde England.* The severity of her expression was a bit unsettling.

She'd come, as they all do, to wallow in the sad history of the Brontë sisters. An estate agent from Keighley rented Clifford Grange to her from September through December. He put Molly in touch with me. I met her in the lounge of the Black Bull and we agreed to the terms of my employment. She needed help setting up housekeeping. She was awaiting the release of her dog from quarantine by Immigration. "Our dog, Tornado," she said. No word about a husband, though I noticed her wedding band.

As we walked up the steep hill, she asked about Clifford Grange. I explained the top of Haworth was once farmland with a large granary and house owned by the Clifford family. About then we passed Haworth Church. I asked, "Have you been inside St. Michael's yet?"

She replied, "Yes, it's the church where the father of the Brontës was pastor so many years."

"Dreary old place, isn't it?"

She showed some animation for the first time. "You're right, it is a morbid place. The Brontë Parsonage, where they all lived, is less dreary, though the graveyard is right beside it."

We went up the last cobbled street in Haworth, where a wuthering wind blew and chased the clouds across the sky like the hounds of heaven. As we approached the house, she asked, "Norah, what do you know about the Clifford family? Are any of their descendants still living?"

I told her all the Cliffords were dead and gone. Indeed, Clifford Grange dates from 1845 and is not a popular rental. Too exposed to the weather in wintertime.

II
Mrs. Molly Lightfoot's Notebook entered in Evidence

September 7
After a wretched week without Tornado, he's finally been released. He keeps me company—settles my nerves better than any doctor's drug. This sabbatical leave may not be the cure I intended, because I've made a thrilling discovery. There are two gaping seams in the bedroom baseboard that appear to be a hiding place. I was seized with the impulse to look inside. To my amazement, I found a bundle of letters in brittle envelopes addressed to Emily Jane Brontë, Haworth Parsonage, Keighley, West Yorkshire. They are signed Ethan Clifford and dated 1846. I began to tremble when I realized they were love letters. I haven't read all of them yet because the ink has faded to pale brown.

If they are authentic, they should be the subject of a book. At the very least, I should write an article, even though I'm not a British Lit scholar. I must find out all about Ethan Clifford—his name suggests Heathcliff. If he is Heathcliff's prototype, what a wonderful discovery! The winter won't be so lonesome now that I have a research project to help me forget the pain my darling Joel suffered before the end.

September 25
Gained access to the complete collection of papers and artifacts at the Brontë Museum after a phone call to Oklahoma. My department head faxed confirmation of my credentials. After two weeks of reading museum documents, I found no mention of Ethan Clifford. My heart sank as I scanned the research materials. However, having read all Ethan's letters now, I can say without a doubt, he loved Emily and met her often on the solitary walks she took on the moors.

On doctor's orders I'm supposed to give my nervous system a rest. Ha! Doctor Barrows should see me now, kept awake by thoughts of proving my discovery that Emily Brontë knew a man's love. Her authorship of *Wuthering Heights* will never be questioned again. One letter reads:

> *Dearest Emily Jane,*
>
> *Do you recall as I do the summer days we wandered across the hills, breathing the scents of flowers only you can call by name, my clever botanist. Speed the day you finish writing your book and walk on the moors with me again. The granite stones where we sat together will be waiting and I will, too, steady as the rock. When I'm there in our favourite place, a breeze whispers my name, using your sweet voice. I long to take you home to Clifford Grange.*
>
> *Forever, Ethan*

His handwriting is so well-drawn, so economical in style, I've almost fallen in love with him, too. I'm seeing a local doctor to renew my Valium prescription.

October 1

How will I cope? Dr. Thornton refused to prescribe Valium, though I showed him the prescription from home. He put me off for four weeks saying, "See how you get on without them." He prescribed long walks instead—the advice of one hundred years ago! I do walk for an hour during the warmest part of the day, otherwise there's mist all morning and it gets so chilly later.

October 3

After five weeks in this house I'm feeling more at home. I'm having Norah come only once a week to clean—Tornado sheds year round.

My progress on the love letters is promising. I know Ethan's hand so well, I have a sense of his presence in my bedroom, most clearly in the heavy dents in the wood floorboards. The room I sleep in must have been his bedroom. Wherever my eye falls I see the marks of a man's boot heels. When the moon is full I open the curtains and invite the light to shine on them. I wonder was he heavy enough to make those dents? Then I realize: of course, he was carrying a woman in his arms. I don't imagine the woman was Emily Brontë—she was a tiny person, dead at the age of thirty. She had caught a chill three months earlier at the funeral of her brother Branwell, only thirty-one when he died, an alcoholic. Haworth Parsonage suffered from the most awful dampness, and possibly worse, being built on a slope down from the graveyard. The soil would be full of disease.

October 9

Spoke with the vicar at St. Michael's. Mr. Dunbarr must be seventy but he has a roof-raising voice. Not the type of man one confides in, though I was prepared to tell him about finding a literary treasure. When I telephoned, I asked about the family at Clifford Grange. He had already checked church records when I arrived and told me that Ethan Clifford never married. Then he showed me Ethan's gravestone in the cemetery. It reads:

ETHAN CLIFFORD
1810 - 1879
For the moors where the linnet is trilling
Its song on the old granite stone
Where the lark the wild skylark was filling
Every breast with delight like its own

Mr. Dunbarr said, "As I remember my local history, there used to be a merchant named Clifford in town—a stationer—you know, writing papers, pens and ink, inkstands. A good business in those days."

Filled with excitement I walked the cobbled streets of Haworth hunting what might have been a stationery. The old shops that are crowded together below the Black Bull cater to the local people as well as to tourists; many selling souvenirs imprinted with images of the Brontë sisters. The pavement is narrow, one person wide, and women doing their shopping came marching down on me with bags and baskets. I was forced into the gutter and turned my ankle on the cobblestones—barely able to walk home. I'm so frustrated by this setback. I couldn't find Clifford's shop in that maze of narrow buildings! But I mustn't get in a frenzy worrying about time passing, or my failure to find something out about Ethan Clifford.

October 15

My ankle heals as I immerse myself in the collected poems of Emily Brontë. To my delight I found the lines on Ethan's tombstone about the skylark and the linnet. Yesterday I went to the cemetery and took photographs of his gravestone to prove Ethan had loved the moors as much as Emily. Thirty years after her death he chose her poem rather than a line from scripture. I hope no one noticed me; I've told no one, not my housekeeper, not even my department head in Oklahoma, about the treasure trove of letters.

Soon as this terrible rainstorm passes, I'm going to buy a case of wine. I was careless to let myself run out before the storm started three days ago. I've been imprisoned here. I pace the downstairs like an animal—front door to back and round and round the dining table. I've never been so restless.

November 2

I called the University of York, asked for the Nineteenth Century British Literature Department. I told the faculty member who answered that I'd found letters to Emily Brontë. I admitted Brontë scholarship is not my specialty; I'm in Twentieth Century American Lit. The man laughed out loud. He said, "The natives of Haworth must have seen you coming and forged them! Some Yorkshire folk have a wild idea of what's funny." I kept my cool and told him about the grave marker inscribed with Brontë's poem. He laughed louder and said something about Americans being overeager.

I lost it. "You'll be laughing out of the other side of your face when I publish my research, dimwit!"

There are other universities I can call, but I need to learn more about Ethan Clifford. I plan to ask at the Hall of Records in Keighley: Did he ever serve on the county council? Was he in the Royal Navy or Army? Ever appear in a court of law? What about his stationery store business? Which bank did he use? What tailoring firm made his clothes? Is his photograph still at the back of some photographer's file in Keighley? More than anything, I'd love to find a photo of him.

November 3

After lunch yesterday I decided to walk with Tornado to Keighley. By the time I walked three miles back home, I was half-frozen and ready to collapse. There are two photographers in Keighley but neither had pictures on file going back that far. I feel terribly let down, my hopes had been so high. In desperation I went to see Dr. Thornton but again he refused to prescribe Valium. When I pleaded with him, he said I must be addicted. Such prejudice! He thinks that only because I'm an American Indian.

November 10

I've decided to turn over Ethan's letters to the Brontë Museum, but first I'm transcribing them into a notebook. It's thrilling to puzzle out his sentences, dashed off like a man sure of what he wants to say. There are hints that his beliefs are like mine—he writes of Nature the way some people write about God. I think he kept writing to Emily because he realized she felt as he did. Like me, she was spiritual, not religious; she habitually ran away from people calling at the parsonage. She baked the daily bread for the household—Pastor Brontë, Branwell, sisters Anne and Charlotte. Worst of all, Branwell needed her to hide his sins from their father, who kept busy writing sermons behind closed doors.

November 16

Weather this week has been abysmal. A northern gale blows all night sending roof tiles crashing to the ground. I can't sleep for puzzling in my mind the reason why Emily walked on the moors with Ethan a few times, then, suddenly, never again. Yet he writes as if he loved her as I loved Joel.

My transcription of the love letters is finished. I've reconsidered the best way to handle them and decided to hide them as Ethan wanted. Because Emily hadn't burned them, I guess he wouldn't either. She never loved Ethan as I loved Joel. His rough laugh brings this drafty house to life for me. Every room echoes with his footsteps as he follows me from room to room. I set a place for him at the table, where he lingers, sharing my wine.

When the parlor fire is hottest and casts long shadows, he takes off his clothes and stands with his back to the fire. His shoulders slope in the sinuous lines of heartbreaking memory. Now he dwells in the vastness beyond, just over the horizon, where the sun rises. He wants me to join him there. I'm tempted to go with him when the sun comes up. If not tomorrow morning, then soon.

November 31

Melancholy confronts me everywhere. Worked on a poem, The He-Soul.

> Airborne, a he-soul chills the house
> when night falls on All Souls
> and the dead who laughed loud in life
> complain with mouths like holes.
> Moaning, like a sough of wind
> half-felt upon the skin,
> conveys the weight of loneliness
> he bears beyond the veil.
> Loss of touch, of taste, of hearing
> fill the he-soul's lamentation,
> a dirge of endless torment
> from the bloodless icy void.
> "Lover, invite me, entrance me," he cries,
> "entangle my being around with your eyes."
> So, yearning for life's dance once more
> His longing sounds a rattle at the door.

Testimony of Mrs. Norah Barnacle

Imagine my shock when I arrived at the front door and heard that beast of a dog howling inside and, on the doorstep, a quart of milk sitting where the milkman had left it on Monday. *Something terrible has happened,* I told myself. Molly Lightfoot was nowhere to be found, her coat and gloves gone. No coffee had been made. Upstairs her notebook lay open on the writing table. Alongside were photos taken in the churchyard. All her books about the Brontë sisters lay scattered about. I looked into her notebook to see what she'd done. Well, it made queer reading, I'll tell you! The unfortunate widow—Archie Gault, the estate agent, told me her husband died recently—conceived the notion that she and Emily Brontë were kindred spirits. The notebook was filled with love letters she wrote to Emily and signed with the name of the man who once lived in this house, Ethan Clifford.

Some don't agree but I believe the spirits of the dead are all around us in old places and they make themselves felt somehow, if you're receptive and open to them, as Molly Lightfoot was, poor woman.

Accidentally on Purpose

by

Ann Marie Curtis

The gun went off in her hand before she realized she had pulled the trigger. She looked down at it with surprise and watched as it fired again.

"Margaret?"

She looked up and saw David in front of her, his hands clutching his chest, his eyes wide with shock. Dropping the gun, she ran to catch him as he fell.

"Oh dear God, David!" She grabbed his shoulders and eased him to the floor. "It was an accident!" her voice quivered. "I didn't mean to shoot you. Please David, forgive me."

He lifted blood-soaked hands away from his shirt. Trembling, he fumbled with the buttons trying to see the wound.

"Wait! Let me get something to stop the bleeding." Margaret gently lowered him to the floor, then hurried to the adjoining bathroom. The white towels were neatly arranged on racks, stamped with the name of the motel. Since they were well-worn, she grabbed them all, kicking the used ones on the floor out of the way. When she returned to the room she saw David weakly reaching for the phone.

"David, dear, you mustn't move," she said rushing around the bed. Margaret pulled a bloody pillow from the bed and placed it under his head. She then folded two of the towels and pressed them against the wound in David's chest.

"Margaret, please..." he murmured, stretching fingers toward the phone.

"Shhh. You must lie still," she said grabbing his hand. "Don't try to talk. I can't believe this happened. I love you, David. I love you so much. It was an accident. I don't even remember putting that gun in my bag. I was so worried when I couldn't find you today. The receptionist at your office said you had an appointment this afternoon. But I don't remember you mentioning an appointment this morning before you left. You usually tell me when you'll be out of the office. We always tell each other our plans for the day.

"Margaret...for the love of God," David tried to grab her arm with his other hand, his blood dulling the tangerine color of her sweater.

"Shush, shush, my darling. You must save your strength," she replied. "We've always been there for each other. We've been in love since the first day we met, haven't we? Do you remember that day? I was just eighteen, barely out of high school when you went to work for Daddy." She gazed across the mess on the bed to the window. The curtains were pulled, letting in streams of the late evening light.

"You were so handsome. You had the most beautiful tan that made your blond hair shine like a halo. And your eyes! They were so blue, like the sky in autumn. Not that they aren't still wonderful, David," she added, looking back at him. "But then," she glanced out the window again, "then you were like an Arthurian knight in shining armor coming to rescue me from my dull life. We were the talk of this whole town. People said we were the perfect Southern couple. Except for those jealous busybodies..." She felt an anguished furrow crease her brow as she began to gently rock him in her arms.

"Such stupid, mean-spirited women—talking behind my back as if they didn't have the sense to know what they were saying. They were trying to belittle our love by implying you were only marrying me because of Daddy's money."

David groaned and tried to pull his hand from her grasp.

"Hush, my darling..." She said as she ran her fingers through his hair. "I didn't pay any mind to those witches. I knew you loved me for myself. Even Daddy tried to warn me. But I got my way, as I always have. I could see your love for me shining from those wonderful blue eyes. And your kisses—no man could ever kiss me the way you do or make love to me so tenderly and not love me. Only me. That's true, isn't it David?"

He tried to raise a hand to grab the towels.

"Oh, my love, how thoughtless of me. Your towels are soaked. Let me put fresh ones on—we must stop the bleeding." She removed the bright red towels, neatly folded two more and placed them against the wound, buttoning his shirt to hold them. "There now, isn't that better?" It really was naughty of you to leave this afternoon without telling me where you were going. I wouldn't normally have minded, but it's happened so often lately."

She glanced at the faded curtains, fake wood paneling, worn pink and orange cushions and frayed lampshades. "I can't imagine why you'd come here. The decor is really quite tacky. We've been very blessed, haven't we? Only the best for us."

David had grown still and his breathing was shallow. She kissed the hand she was holding, then kissed his forehead. "Are you feeling better now? I found out about your appointments by accident—you know I'd never intentionally snoop. You remember the charity carnival at St. Matthew's elementary school that I'm hosting with Lucille Owens? Well, I called to see if we could borrow the 36 cup coffeemaker from the office but the receptionist said you were out. Like today, you hadn't mentioned it at breakfast that day. I brushed that time aside as an oversight on your part, but the next time it happened I began to wonder."

He twitched slightly.

"Are you cold, darling? Let me get you a blanket." She pulled the blood-splattered bedspread to the floor and gently tucked it around him. "Is that better? Mustn't let you catch a cold."

The worn carpet threads scratched her face as she put her face near his. "It seemed every time I told you I had a meeting, you always had an appointment away from the office. I love you and I do trust you, but in the back of my mind I kept hearing those terrible things people said about you. So...this morning I told a little white lie about a club meeting this afternoon. I knew you'd forgive me. You do forgive me, don't you darling? I waited outside your office to see where you'd go. First that fake Janet Windom came out—I really don't see why you and Daddy hired her. She may do wonders for the company but she has as much class as those cheerleaders back in high school. No one with the country club would ever think to ask her to sit on a committee. Her taste in clothes–I mean a pink blouse with a red suit, pants at that! Anyway..." She looked closely at him. He didn't seem to be breathing. She poked him gently. "David, are you listening? Sometimes I think you're not listening to me when I talk." Shifting positions, she leaned against the bed with her knees pulled to her chin.

"Anyway, as I was saying, shortly after she left, you came out carrying your briefcase–the one I had engraved for you on our eighth wedding anniversary. The gold lettering has held up beautifully, hasn't it darling?" She gently caressed his brow. "I followed your car when you left. Please don't think badly of me, but it really was easy. Imagine my surprise when you drove out of town to this tawdry motel in Muskogee. I thought it might be a legitimate meeting until I saw you go into this room without your briefcase."

Margaret stood and began pacing in front of the bed. She glanced at the bed and then at her husband.

"Why, David, why? I work so hard to be the perfect wife. I keep the house clean, cook your favorite food, entertain your clients and do charity work so you'll look good to the people in town. What more could I have done? Tell me where I failed!"

Only the knocking of the air conditioner broke the silence. She impatiently kicked David's foot. "Answer me! At least I deserve an explanation!" She kneeled next to him, his blood cold on her knees as she shook him by his collar. "I told Daddy to give you those promotions. Did you really think you were smart enough to earn them? It was me! Me who paid for the house, me who paid for that car outside. My pride, my dignity, and all those years of wanting you to love me. And this...this is what I get in return?" She let go of him and stood. Sirens in the distance were growing closer. Finding the gun, she picked it up with shaking hands.

"You're a sorry excuse for a man, David Mitchell! Love and honor 'till death do us part—what a crock! I should have listened to those witches and my father. You used me. People have been laughing at me behind my back for years, haven't they? Poor Margaret...poor little Margaret." She fired, barely wincing as David's body jumped from the impact. "I hate you! Do you hear me, I hate you!" Again she fired, then watched the thin trail of smoke float gently across the bed as it swirled in the current blown by the air conditioner.

After a few moments she lowered the gun and dropped it. The sirens grew louder. She glanced at her watch and straightened clothes. "David, don't forget we have the Drummonds coming over for dinner this evening. Daddy wants you to go over the proposal for them." Picking up her purse, she took out a tissue to wipe her hands as she looked back at the room with a smile. "I'll just wait outside while you get dressed, darling. And please, Ms. Windom," she said as she glanced at the woman lying on the bed, her dull eyes staring blankly at the ceiling, the blood crusting around the bullet wound in her neck, "do join us. I don't believe you have been to our home and I'm sure David would like to introduce you to the Drummonds. I do love entertaining his clients and he has so many...I'm so proud of him."

Taking out a compact, she powdered her nose. "I'm truly sorry about your blouse, but really, pink with red? Well," Margaret added with a smile, "at least most of the blouse matches the suit now. Don't take too long."

The door clicked behind her as cars screeched to a halt outside, their sirens suddenly stilled.

It's All in the Perspective
by
Robert Avery Clemens

Though my eyes remained closed, the heat on my body and the wine-red color of the interior of my eyelids told me the morning sun was shining through my bedroom window. I reached for the extra pillow and covered my face.

The doorbell rang again and again I ignored it. At the third ring, I groaned, threw the pillow aside, rolled out of bed and struggled into the jeans I'd dropped on the floor the night before. Combing my hair with the fingers of one hand while I rubbed sleep from my eyes with the other, I went to the speaker in the hallway and pushed the talk button.

"Yeah. Who is it?"

"It's Becky, you doofus. Who'd you think it was this hour of the morning?"

"What time is it?" I asked.

"It's seven-thirty. Look, little brother, I'm standing at your front door loaded down with buckets, mops, brooms, and every kind of detergent known to the cleaning industry. Do you think we might wait to hold this conversation until you've seen fit to let me in?"

"Sure. Be right there."

I walked down the hall, punched the code on the alarm panel, unlocked the front door and stepped back. Becky struggled to drag the cleaning supplies into the entryway before the storm door closed. She didn't make it. The door swung and snagged the ends of the mops and brooms.

She was effectively caught, neither in nor out. With an accusing look she said, "You could help, you know."

I pushed the storm door back and took the more awkward items from her— the mops, brooms and plastic buckets. "I'm sorry, Becky. I'm not with it yet. I just rolled out of bed."

She gave me the once over. "You look it. A night on the town?"

I yawned. "Naw, just couldn't sleep."

"Second thoughts?"

"Yes...no. Maybe. Where's Jack?"

"He went to drop the kids off at his mother's and pick up something for breakfast."

The fact that Becky had referred to me as 'little brother' seemed totally incongruous once we were standing together in the kitchen. Becky's a good eight inches shorter than I. We do look alike, though. We have the same dark, curly hair and blue eyes. She feels she has the right to call me 'little brother' because I'm the youngest.

"You know what I think?" she asked, depositing her armload of cleaning supplies on the counter. "I think you're being way too hasty with this stupid project. You're not sure you've lost Rachel."

"Rachel's been gone over six months," I argued. "She's not coming back." I leaned the mops and brooms in the corner by the door and set the buckets beside them.

"I can tell she's been gone by the look of this kitchen," Becky said disparagingly. "So…you're going through with your plan to completely gut the house, paint, and install new carpet and furniture?"

I had started toward my bedroom to find shoes, socks and a shirt. "Yep, that's pretty much it," I called over my shoulder. "Can't bring a new woman in here with memories of Rachel cluttering up the place." I realized I was baiting her. Becky was very fond of Rachel.

She followed me into the bedroom. "Do you have a new woman?"

"Well…no. But if I did…"

Becky planted herself in the doorway, her hands on her hips, assuming what her husband, Jack, calls her 'discussion' stance. I braced myself to rebutt an argument in Rachel's favor that I'd already heard many times.

"Paul Matthews, you know Rachel was the logical one to return home to help her parents through the family crisis when her sister, Peggy, was so terribly hurt in the car wreck that killed her husband. You know that."

"Yeah. I don't…I can't fault Rachel for that. But Peggy's pretty much recovered now." I pulled yesterday's T-shirt over my head and sat on the edge of the bed to slip on socks and shoes. "Rachel's a small town girl, Becky. I'm thinking she's had her fling in the city. I know her parents didn't approve of us living together. I'm guessing they've talked her into staying in the town where she grew up, maybe settling down, marrying a local boy, and having a house full of kids."

"So…*you* don't want to marry and have kids."

"I'm just not in a big hurry to be tied down," I said rather defensively.

"Same thing."

"No, it's not! I want to get married. I want to have kids. It's just that I can think of a lot of things I'd like to do with Rachel before marriage and kids slow us down."

"Have you told Rachel that?"

I stood, shrugged. "Not in so many words."

Becky sighed. Her hands fell to her sides. "Look, Paul…Maybe once Rachel was away for a while she began to wonder if you were really serious about her?"

"Why should she think that? I've *begged* her to come home."

"Yeah—*over the phone.* Allow me to make a wild-assed guess here…"

Since there was no way I could stop her, I replied, "Fire away."

"I think, somehow, both of you got your feelings hurt. Now, you're both too darned stubborn to make the first move."

"Sounds about right," I admitted. "When Rachel first brought up the idea of leaving her job in Kansas City to return home to care for her sister, I probably wasn't properly supportive. My only excuse is, I wasn't really aware of just how ill her sister was at the time. Now that Peggy is so much better, I feel abandoned–especially when I wake at night and Rachel's not at my side."

"Long, lonely nights can make a person lose perspective, Paul. Don't do this thing right now. Wait until both of you start thinking straight again. Then maybe you can do it together."

"Too late. I've already bought carpet–which will be installed later this week–and a truckload of new furniture. I've made arrangements for Goodwill to pick up my old stuff and I've rented a storage unit for Rachel's things."

I could tell Becky was preparing to attack from a different angle. Luckily, the doorbell interrupted us. Opening the door, I let my brother-in-law inside as I said, "Saved by the bell."

Jack grinned. "Becky been giving you a hard time?"

I grunted.

"Women," he said. "Can't live with 'em, can't live without 'em." He handed me a gallon of milk and a dozen donuts as we headed for the kitchen.

While the three of us ate, I mapped out the weekend's chores. Becky was to pack the breakables while Jack and I carried the furniture I wanted to keep out to Rachel's side of the garage–the empty side. We'd haul her stuff directly to the storage unit in Jack's pickup. The really ratty stuff would go into the dumpster parked in the driveway. Once all the rooms were cleared, we'd have to paint before the carpet installation crew arrived. I didn't expect to get it all done in two days. I had two weeks vacation along with Becky's promise to help during the day and Jack's offer to help every evening he was free.

I had come by my house through a piece of luck. Bad luck for Great Uncle Charles, a confirmed bachelor who had died five years earlier; good luck for me, since as his 'homeless' nephew I had inherited the house while Becky inherited his liquid assets. The all brick house was not large, but was tidily efficient with a kitchen, dining room, living room, family room, three bedrooms and two baths crammed into less than eighteen hundred square feet. The jalousie-windowed sun porch was the perfect place to view the fenced lot of tall trees and mature landscaping. I had grown to love the place and I thought Rachel had, too. However, there was no denying that Uncle Charlie had let the interior deteriorate, and Rachel and I had done nothing to improve the situation. When my 'stuff' and her 'stuff' were added to the eclectic mix Uncle Charlie had left me, the place resembled an overstocked secondhand store. Since Rachel left, I'd had more than enough time to assess the mess and had decided to do something about it.

With the milk and donuts half-consumed, and Jack and Becky–while not in complete agreement with my plans–still willing to help, we got down to business.

I pushed them hard. No surprise then, that pleading exhaustion they left early, around five o'clock. I showered, ate the leftovers from breakfast and lunch, then retired to the nearly empty living room. I turned on the TV—housed in the large entertainment cabinet Rachel and I had picked out together—and turned to CNN. Sprawled in Uncle Charlie's well-worn leather recliner, I found myself bone-tired with every fleeting thought fixating on Rachel.

We'd met at the advertising agency where I worked as head of the art department. She appeared at my office door one particularly busy morning and stood waiting politely for me to notice her. When I set aside the proofs I'd been examining and looked up, she asked, "Are you Paul Matthews?"

"Guilty," I replied.

She came inside and placed a single sheet of paper on my cluttered desk. "This was with the last group of purchase orders you sent to accounting," she said. "Apparently, you missed it. At any rate, since you didn't okay it, Ms. Gardner sent me to ask if you would take the time to approve it now."

I was looking at the quintessential country girl...ripe, luscious figure, long tightly curled hair pinned at the nape of her neck—the color more copper than gold—hazel eyes set wide in a neat, heart-shaped face. Her complexion was perfect, clear peaches and cream color seldom seen in redheads, but all the more striking because of its rarity. Nice. Very nice.

"And who might you be?" I asked.

She colored ever so slightly. "Rachel Atkins. I'm one of Ms. Gardner's assistants."

"You must be new."

"I am. I just started work last week."

"Ah...I see." I reached for the paper, looked it over, signed it, and handed it back. "Welcome to Jackson-Polander."

"Thank you."

As she left, I couldn't help but notice that her backside looked great, too.

The following weeks, I regularly missed signing at least one purchase order in every stack that I sent upstairs. Just as regularly, Ms. Gardner sent Rachel to chastise me for my inattentiveness. During that time I managed to learn a great deal about her—she came from a rather large family, most of whom still lived in or near her hometown in central Missouri, the job with the agency was her first job in the city, she was single with no current boyfriend, she lived in an apartment north of the river with a couple of female roommates she suspected might be gay, and no, she herself was not gay.

Eventually, Ms. Gardner caught on to me and started sending a different assistant—a nice enough young woman, just not Rachel. After several days of missing her, I gathered the current stack of purchase orders from my desk and headed for the twenty-fifth floor. Dropping them on Ms. Gardner's desk, I said, "Signed." When she looked up, I added, "Every one of them."

"It's about time you got it right," she said.

"I need to talk to Rachel."

Ms. Gardner is a very sharp lady. I braced myself for the sarcasm that I knew was forthcoming.

"Need?" she said. "Need? Oh...really?"

"Yes, really."

She smiled, relenting. "She's in the file room."

Rachel was digging through one of the drawers when she saw him. With a smile she asked, "What brings you to the twenty-fifth floor, Paul?"

I leaned an elbow on the cabinet beside her and waited for her to look up. There was no denying it—she had the most beautiful eyes I'd ever seen. "I seem to have worked up enough nerve to ask you out," I replied. "How about dinner this Friday...dinner and a movie?"

"Doesn't the agency have a rule against fraternization?"

"No. It does have a rule against married couples working here, but there's no rule forbidding employees to date, or oddly enough, even live together."

She smiled. "I see you've done your homework. Yes, I'd love to go out with you."

It was as simple as that. Three months later she moved in with me. Everything was great for almost two years, then the horrible wreck that killed her brother-in-law and almost killed her sister changed our lives forever.

She returned home, leaving me with the gut-wrenching feeling she had also left me.

In the days following Becky's first harangue she hardly let up on me. Other than that, the rehabilitation of the house went smoothly. By Thursday afternoon of the second week of my vacation, virtually everything I'd planned had been accomplished.

Becky left early. I decided I needed a shower.

When I emerged from the bathroom toweling my hair, I found Rachel lying on the new bed clad only in white lace panties and a push-up bra. I froze.

Our eyes met. She smiled, then her gaze drifted downward.

"Becky said you'd be glad to see me," she said.

I tried to cover myself with the towel, but she reached to pull it slowly through my fingers and drop it on the floor.

"She called you, didn't she?" I asked.

"Yes. Are you angry with her?"

I allowed myself to be pulled onto the bed. "No," I replied. "Sometimes my sister can be quite astute."

"By the way," Rachel whispered, just before my mouth covered hers. "I like what you've done with our home."

Memoirs/Personal Essays
First Place

The Lot
by
Rebecca Crandell

Nestled behind my childhood home in Wichita lay a wild wooded area we called 'the lot.' To the casual observer, it was no more than a thick tangle, screening our house from view, yet so much more lived there than vegetation and rocks. The lot was my private retreat—an enchanted region that fed my imagination during the years when life drifted in simplicity.

During the simmering warmth of summertime, I slipped into deep green foliage and disappeared from this world into another. Mysterious and quiet, foreign to adults, it sheltered and nurtured me. A well-hidden path I discovered once led me to a small enclosure made by a circle of skinny trees. This became my sanctuary, where I crafted my first writing and learned the forest's green language. I had not yet read Thoreau or Kipling, but my time in the lot resembled the simple, free existence of *Walden* or *The Jungle Book*. Soon I taught myself how to step without sound through brittle undergrowth—to move against the breeze until I could surprise foraging sparrows. Rather than human intruder, I named myself a creature of the wood, belonging there as much as robins or squirrels.

Here in this earthy, secret atmosphere, I first read C.S. Lewis's *Narnia Chronicles*, and *believed*. While traversing forest paths, I searched for the doorway waiting to whisk me into that magical land. Charms tingled my fingertips and Aslan's golden breath seemed to kiss my cheeks.

Though the lot kept its invisible gateways hidden, it proved generous in other ways. Once, I happened upon a staff, four feet tall and perfectly straight. Worm-sign covered it like druid runes. Another time I unearthed a complete mouse skeleton, airy and fragile, from my enclosure's leaf-carpeted floor.

One of the lot's most valuable, long-lasting gifts was a distinct appreciation of solitude. I learned to lie still, watching the changing cloud patterns through a frame of leaves and branches. Under this fertile canopy, stories crept into my mind like dreams, or voices perhaps, from other lives.

At times, I wonder what happened to my walking stick. The mouse bones crumbled, and my childish stories lay tucked in nostalgia's drawer. Yet the lot remains, after a fashion. When my parents moved, the new owners contained it behind a high cedar fence and chopped down most of the old trees. I wish they had paused to listen first to that elegant, rustling wisdom. Would they still have had courage enough to lift the ax? Landscaped and civilized, the once-wild area now suffocates under benches and flower pots.

If every child had access to a wild, secret place, what would our world be? Having the lot did not prepare me for this life—rather it offered seclusion from it. Indeed, it hindered me from taking my place in the cold city forest. Though I became adult in body, the world's constant blare and metallic essentials battered at my sensibilities. I unconsciously constructed a thick wall to protect myself from the assault. Nonetheless, I will always believe my small piece of land did nurture something tangible. It wrapped me in a cocoon of poetry that tinges every word I write. Because of the lingering effect of those days, I believe writers cannot be social beings in the same way other people can. They must thrive in solitude. They must learn how to listen to unseen things, and they must learn to trust what they hear. My voice came to me under a leafy awning, whispering through the breast of Mother Gaia. Were it not for the lot, as nurturing in its way as a physical mother, I doubt I would be able to write now.

What the lot gave me did not disappear, turn to dust, or molder in a drawer. Graciously it has remained, an integral part of my writing and of me.

Perhaps the lot did allow me through its invisible gateway. For now, even in stark adult reality, the fantasy and magic that first befriended me there, on a tiny plot of wild land in Kansas, remains vivid and alive. A mere thought away.

Memoirs/Personal Essays
Honorable Mention

A River in the Heartland
by
Marla English

It's 4 a.m. Who intentionally gets up this early in the morning? My overactive, know-it-all, must-have-the-last-word mind concludes those who awaken this early are (a) people who have taken on more than they can accomplish in a twenty-four-hour period, and (b) those who have failed to contribute anything of substance to planet earth, except maybe their ability to daydream and watch, as if in a coma, the comings and goings of others...

My thoughts are quickly interrupted. What is that sound outside my bedroom window? I'm not leaving the comfort of my bed for foolishness, so whatever it is, had better be good. As I stand, I slowly begin pulling back these old chantilly lace curtains (old and ugly curtains). Sorry Big Mama. I see a shadow. It's nothing, just a tree limb. Wow...the rain is really coming down. The brisk wind is struggling to make an announcement. I wonder what is so important that it would dare interrupt the orchestra of thunder and rain. Doesn't the wind understand the order of nature? Perhaps not, but it somehow understood my internal dialogue because as soon as I asked the question, the wind ceased to blow. After this odd and beautiful dance of nature, all that remains is a gentle shower. Who knows, at this rate, the sun may grace us with her presence and steal center stage by displaying a rainbow at the water's end. Well, despite this mini concerto, the morning is still somewhat dreary. What good can possibly occur on a day such as this?

I haven't been sleeping well lately. And when I am asleep, I have the same recurring dream. Three old African women, their skin is so shiny and black they almost look blue, are beautifully adorned in regal headdresses, jewelry, and full-length green and gold wraps. Who are they? Why are they at the river's edge? Or are they actually standing in the water? Anyway, I can't shake the feeling that if I could get to the river, they would tell me why they interrupted my sleep yet again. Big Mama used to say it is common sense not to awaken someone who is asleep. That really used to make me laugh. When is the last time I've done that? Laugh, I mean. Oh, let's get back to what people do who have "sense."

On a rainy day I imagine they would stay indoors, pamper themselves (to which my feet would say, "Thank ya, Jesus"), or they'd curl up with a good book. Well...to do things that make sense has never been my way. Having said so, I think today would be a good day to take a trip to the river. Yeah...that's exactly what I need...I need...

The river has always supplied me with a sense of calmness. Because of its vastness, I never felt one ounce of guilt as I poured out the frustrations and sadness of this thing called "my life."

"Man, look at all this water," Big Mama would say. "It's more than enough to cleanse all the sorrows of a man's soul." It seems like a lifetime ago since I heard those words. Why would I remember them today?

As a little girl, I would spend countless hours imagining myself standing at the edge of the riverbank. Forty years later, I still long to do the same. Oh, my goodness, I'm getting off track. Where was I? Oh, I remember. I was talking about my needs. What do I need anyway? Despite the weather—it's really pouring out there—I need to get to the river. I know I should probably wait for a more pleasant day, but everything in me is screaming, "Go...go now." Looking back, how many opportunities have I missed? I have a knack for being in the right place at the wrong time. Um...

Almost fifty years old. Where did the time go? Who invited these wrinkles? Oh, my goodness, is that grey hair at my temple? Are those my thighs making that flapping sound?

I have spent my whole life sick. Sick. No...maybe "ill" is a better word—

I-I, L-lacked, L-love. It's funny, looking back. Frequent hospital visits, medication, and machinery always left me worse off than before. What was all that about? All my life, all I have ever known is...um...you know...I must confess I can't recall, in this moment anyway, what it is I *do* know. Oh, wait...I know an awful lot about misdiagnoses, self-sabotage, sadness, self-pity, and shame. It all tends to follow me like the fat on my hind part. All of this sickness. Does that mean my soul and spirit are sick too?

Big Mama's favorite Scriptures are in the Book of Psalms. How long did that Bible sit in the center of the coffee table? I wonder if Big Mama knew more than one verse of Scripture? I never saw her reading. Come to think of it, had that Bible ever been opened? Too many questions.

Big Mama's gone now. They say one day she sat in that old black rocker, went to sleep, and never woke up. I cried...a lot. I promise you, fifty times a day she used to say, "...leadeth me beside the still rivers of water, Grandbaby, and he will restore Big Mama's soul. Glory to God!"

In this lineage of beautiful, strong, prideful black women within my family, could it be all of our souls and very spirits are in need of restoration? Surely it cannot be that there remains a deeper sickness passed down to our souls, and has contaminated our spirits and gone undetected all these years. How is this possible? Undetected. Is that kinda like the fat around our bellies that simply shows up in our late forties? The fat that's been there all along and one day it just pops out, announces it's staying, and refuses to leave no matter what you do. What do we really know about such things? I never really gave my soul or my spirit the nurturing it needed. How do you say "sorry" for such an oversight? I know...I know...get on with the story.

What should I wear on my trip to the water's edge? My coming out party, if you will. Looking inside this closet, who would imagine beneath this hardened shell is a woman who loves sheer, soft, and boldly bright colors? Remind me again, why did I buy all of this brown, grey, and black? Okay, after today, I promise NO MORE DARKNESS! Could that be a metaphor for life? I know it sounds crazy, especially with the rain, but I've decided I'm going to wear a full-length, bright orange, cotton sun dress with perfectly embroidered little flowers, big hooped earrings, and yes...I'm taking off this wig.

My, how my hair has grown. The chemotherapy was kind. It left me with just enough hair to call myself "curly top." I can hear Big Mama laughing, saying, "Girl, your hair 'bout a minute to one, ain't it?" That was her way of saying how short the length of my hair was. It always made me laugh. I'll wear my black granny boots, grab my oversized army green trench coat, an umbrella, and I'm out the door. River...ready or not...here I come.

Driving today, I suddenly realized how much of a loner I've become, and yet I can't stand silence. More than half my life lived and I'm wondering how much I've missed. What is it I needed to hear all these years that would have changed the woman I see looking back at me in the rearview mirror? Hearing. Hearing is a funny thing. How was I taught to hear? What should I have been listening for? Was it a sound? A voice? And after hearing, what should I do with what I have heard? Too many questions. The day is certainly dreary enough without all of this clutter. I wish my mind would be still. I'm almost there...God help me to simply enjoy the sound of the rain.

Finally...I'm here. Suddenly, I'm very nervous. What has drawn me here to this place at this season of my life? Who will I encounter? What questions will be asked of me? What questions will I...I...never mind. The closer I get to the river's edge, it's as if all of nature ceases activity. No wind. No rain. As I look up, the sun blinks and a rainbow appears on the water. But the rainbow isn't the only thing I see. Suddenly, I see a woman. A reflection. I can't move. How long have I stood here seemingly suspended in time? I attempt to sit. The reflection is looking intently at me and shaking its head. I hear an audible voice speak. "No, please do not sit. It is time for you to stand." Stand? Okay, is she crazy or am I? These two pencils I call legs are not strong enough to stand for any real length of time.

The reflection continues to shake its head. Oh...oh, I get it. You aren't talking about my physical posturing, you're speaking to my inner man. I turn again for the reflection to validate my response and, sure enough, she did. I'm certain, dear reader, you are thinking, What a simple request; just do it. Well, yes, simple it would be if my spirit and soul had not been MIA for the past forty-some odd years. The reflection senses my hesitation.

Oh my God, is she coming up out of the water? Am I dreaming? All my life I've been told something is wrong with my mind. Will this reflection confirm that? Too many questions. I'll quiet so I can hear what she is saying. "Who summoned you here?" Summoned. What is she talking about? I feel ridiculous enough as it is talking to a reflection, so she better be quick about getting to the point. She appears to be unmoved by my agitation. "Why have you allowed the voices of others to be louder than your own? You have spent far too much time running. You were drawn here today to show who you've been running from. Drawn here to face the silent cries of soul and spirit. Finally, you were drawn here to learn about the women who came before you, and understand the woman you are, the woman you are destined to become. Now...be seated."

At this point I don't know if I sat down or fell down, but somehow my bottom made contact with a damp tree stump. She had my undivided attention. "You have spent your entire life wandering from city to country, wandering to the point of extreme excess in your mind. Is that what doctors call 'breakdown?' You're running from love. It is time to stop running. Stop wandering. You are home now. It is not an accident you returned to the land of beginning, to the place where your soul and spirit can finally heal. This is where the weary can rest and the broken can be restored. Welcome. Welcome to the heartland."

It has been many years since I was able to recall the splendor and majesty of home. I can see Big Mama hanging freshly washed sheets on the clothesline. Man, I loved that smell. I often wondered, *How can somebody be so happy hanging sheets?* I never realized how much love went into each one. Father's tilling the ground, preparing it for seed. I stood on the porch and got full just inhaling the aroma from the kitchen. Fresh homemade bread and walnut raisin oatmeal cookies—my two favorites to this day. Life back then was simple. I could stand on this porch for hours just watching Daddy's hands. He gave so much attention to the soil. What was this mysterious hold the land seemed to have on the people back then? Father had such a respect, a reverence almost. He always said, "Take care of it, and it will take care of you." I never understood what he meant, but I always smiled real big and acted like I did.

It's funny to think about hands. Big Mama's hands nurtured, spanked, cleaned, baked, taught, played the piano (she taught herself), and made our Sunday dresses. To this day, I can't figure how hands that made cream puffs could spank so hard when we were disobedient or caught lying. Today, we take telling a lie so lightly. Back then, if you lied, your behind was mad at you for weeks because it couldn't sit down. Trust me, I know. The people back then were different—friendly, hard workers. They always looked you right in the eye when they spoke. Daddy said if a person couldn't look you in the eye, except he was blind, then don't trust them. And years later, Daddy, I must confess you were right. Thank God for the wisdom that came out of the Heartland.

My dad had hunting dogs. We were not allowed to play with them. Daddy said it would make them "soft." My favorite memory was riding in Dad's old, beat-up truck with him and Mother. Daddy's best friend was killed, they say he was going too fast and my dad was in the backseat. Since that day, Daddy has never driven. I know it made him sad, but it wasn't his fault. He wasn't even driving. That was Daddy's way. "Some things you just don't talk about." So we didn't.

I loved our truck. Wherever we went, you heard us long before you saw us. I would play for hours once Dad was finished hunting, because then I could sit beside him, eat my bologna and cheese sandwich, play in the dirt, and help put a worm on the pole. Man, those were the best times of my life. Eating my sandwich and staring at the water—life couldn't get much better than this.

Everything happens so quickly as I sit at the water's edge. The reflection (I call her "She") continued to plow away at my troubled spirit and wounded soul. Suddenly, a most glorious event is occurring; the river's current is changing. I'm getting dizzy. Too much information. Too many revelations. I feel so naked. I want to run, to hide. I can't. This time I must…I must stand and face TRUTH. My God, this is painful. Old mindsets, memories, behaviors, and beliefs are leaving me. My soul and spirit are being purged. The reflection spoke, "I cannot be new wine in an old wineskin." I can't explain how it is possible to feel so much fire amidst so much water, but I think after it's all over I'll finally be okay. With my head down in my hands, I hear her say, "You come from a land, a community, a body of builders and believers, visionaries. Those who had a genuine love for country. Those who honored family. Committed folk. People of integrity. Heroes. Adventurers. Warriors. Those able to identify and operate in any season. A prepared people full of insight and wisdom, simple folk who said what they meant and meant what they said. Who understood working together to accomplish a common goal. A handshake was a covenant, more valuable than the spoken or written word. Not only were they builders, but they were humble people always willing to rebuild if their foundation was proven faulty. They reverenced God—a thankful people. They had very little and yet possessed great wealth."

I am speechless. I can't process all that is being revealed to me. How could I have been so reckless with such a rich heritage? She continued, "The people of the heartland, of which you are, understood order, sacrifice. They were a determined people. Unselfish. Now…who are you? What are you prepared to leave to those who will come after you? The women understood timing. Remember Big Mama? How many times did she say to you, 'Even creation got enough sense to know there is a time for everything.'" I hated to admit it, but I didn't remember until she spoke it. Where had my memory been all these years? "You're a singer. Why aren't you singing? You're a very funny person. Why aren't you sharing your joy with others? You come from a long line of those who laughed from their soul, and out of that same soul came music."

I attempted to interrupt her to tell her of my woes. She stopped me. "You are foolish if you believe these people did not endure hardship, uncertainty, disappointment, and pain. These were not perfect women. They hid to protect. They denied to maintain their sanity. They played the lesser and the weaker to make others greater and strong. In the end, they did the best they knew how, for, you see, there was no one to teach them differently. Knowing that, it's time for you to grow up and get on with the business of living. These women understood and because of this, their action or inaction greatly impacted more than themselves. You come from such women. They viewed the land not only as a place of planting, but considered their very spirit, soul, and body a land needing cultivating, watering, and washing until it returned home to Jesus. You became barren when you failed to give back to the land, so it would sustain you in your seasons of drought."

I want to cry. I want someone to hold me and make it all go away. She looked at me as if sensing my thoughts. I wait for a comforting word. She spoke, "Listen closely, it will be dark soon." Hello. I said, I'm hurting. Could a "sista" get some comfort? "That's manipulation, emotional blackmail; or it would be if I bought into it. Stop performing. Those behaviors are rooted out of fear. Why are you afraid?" ...ouch, I—"you were not created to fear nor were you created to carry past, present, or future burdens—neither yours nor anyone else's. You bought into a lie. There is nothing wrong with your mind. It is your mind-set that is in error." Isn't mind and mindset one and the same, I asked. "No," she replied. "Your problem all these years has been where you have allowed your mind to go." Oddly enough, I understood. The years of confusion, bitterness, shame, and unforgiveness slowly begin to leave. I was the gatekeeper of my mind. I determined where it would go, what it would think. How stupid of me to entrust such a precious gift into the hands of fools (self included). God, I know you have forgiven me, please help me to forgive myself.

I was waiting for the reflection to acknowledge what I said, but...she didn't. Well, not exactly. She began with, "The women of the Heartland understand something about time that you must learn to tap into." Have I mentioned she had gotten on my last nerve? Well for the record, she had. "You were forgiven the moment you asked. Now let's move on." And that was all she said. After all was revealed to me, up to this point, was I still trying to evoke sympathy? I probably was (smile).

"The women of the heartland lived surrendered lives. Knowing that, you, too, must surrender. They are women who gave birth or produced fruit always in its proper season. Whatever they laid their hands on was blessed. What are you producing? What are you giving birth to? Do you understand?" I nodded. Yes. "You must learn to let go of dead things (people, places). Release your troubles, your uncertainty, your secret rage, your insecurity, and your fears. You were created to produce life. Stand up. Hold your head high. You don't justly serve those who have came before you by playing small. Release all you have been holding hostage. And while you're at it, release your spirit and your soul. It's time for you to live, girl. Let it go. Now...breathe!"

It'd been a long day. Where had the time gone? The sun had gone down. As I look up, the reflection slowly fades. I immediately jump up and scream, "No...no...Wait! You haven't answered my questions. You can't just leave me here." And as quickly as I uttered those words, she was gone! I'm stunned. Suddenly I hear a small voice say, "Look . . . look in the water." Still shaken, I went to the water and looked in. I don't understand. The only person I see is ME!

I now hear yet another familiar voice. This time it's Big Mama's. "Baby, when you was a little girl, the townspeople called you L'il River. When your spirit said, 'Come to the River,' you didn't need to come here. River isn't a place. You... baby...are River. And all we wanted was for you to come...to yourself."

Memoirs/Personal Essays
Honorable Mention

The Smokehouse
by
Melody Sullivan

We called it "the smokehouse." I really didn't know why. It was an old small building that stood a few yards from the backdoor of the farmhouse we lived in from the time I was six years old until I was eight. The paint on the smokehouse was almost gone and the multitude of varied spaces between the boards turned it into a puzzle of sorts. It had no electricity. It didn't lock from the inside, but it stayed closed as long as the small piece of wood screwed onto the outside of the door was turned horizontally across the doorjamb. I never saw anyone go in or come out.

I was the oldest of four children, so you can imagine what my mother must have gone through, having four kids in six years. You can also imagine that on some summer days our small house seemed entirely too tiny for her to share with four little ones while my father spent long hours tending fields of spinach and green beans he grew for sale to our small town's cannery.

The summer after I finished the first grade of school was when I discovered what my mom thought was an ideal use for the smokehouse. Before that, we weren't allowed in it under any circumstances. But one day, when I was being especially difficult, she decided the perfect punishment would be a few minutes in the smokehouse by myself until I was ready to behave.

Having never been in there before, I expected the worst—though I had no idea what the worst was. Mother sternly escorted me to the door, unlocked it, and asked me to step inside. Then she locked the door from the outside, and said she would return in five minutes to see if I had come to my senses.

At first I was a little worried, but plenty of sunlight shone in between the boards. Also, the spaces were ample enough to allow a comfortable breeze throughout the whole place. Who needed electricity? I decided to do a little exploring. After all, I had five whole minutes! I quickly discovered the smokehouse held a few forbidden pleasures.

After a cursory check of the interior, I had my five-minute plan in place. I found several piles of old comic books and some intriguing looking detective magazines. But first I had to get comfortable. I located a long padded bench seat that had been pulled out of a bus or something. It had some torn places, but was plenty long enough for a six-year-old to lie on and made a perfect reading place. I pulled the seat by the door, where the best sunlight was, and lay down with my

55

reading stash.

I started with the detective magazines, because they had real pictures and looked more interesting than the comics. Were they ever! Back in the 1950's, detective magazines were pretty risqué, and even after forty-six years, I still remember the title of my favorite detective story—"Pretty, Pregnant, and Plugged." As a six-year-old, I had no clue what "pregnant" or "plugged" meant and could barely sound out the words, but the pictures in that story fascinated me!

The beautiful woman in the black and white close-up photo on the first page of the story had long dark hair, and she wore expensive-looking earrings. She was smiling and looking over her naked shoulder straight at me. When I turned the page, she was wearing a stripper costume with nothing on top except what looked like a couple of small buttons with ribbons attached. (Gasp!) When I turned another page, she wore a skirt and blouse, but she was bent over at the waist so that I couldn't see her face. It appeared to me she'd been shot several times, judging from the blood splattered around her. I don't remember who shot her, or why...

In no time at all, my mom was outside the door asking if I had learned my lesson and was ready to rejoin society. In fact, I wasn't ready to give up this oasis of privacy and comfort. I told her I needed a little more time. She said she'd be back in two minutes, and I better be ready by then!

Two minutes gave me loads of time to put everything back in its original place, so when she opened the door I was standing with the appropriate "sorry for my sins" attitude. She gave me a hug and apologized for having to punish me, but maybe I would know better next time.

I've never told mom what a great place the smokehouse was, and it honestly made me a worse kid than I would have been if she hadn't put me in there. When I needed a break from my sister and two younger brothers, I could always figure out some way to get put back in. I looked at my favorite detective story every single time, too.

I've never discovered who put the magazines there. But one of these days, I'm going to ask my dad if he ever got put in the smokehouse!

Feature Magazine Articles
First Place

A Tall Tale in Tahlequah:
Mr. Ed's Final Resting Place
by
Maria DeLong

No one visits Mister Ed's gravesite by accident. On a windswept prairie north of Tahlequah a granite monument is laid over an inconspicuous mound of grass. The limbs of a wild cherry tree provide faint shade, and a cross-hatch stall evokes memories of the days when the talented palomino roamed the seventeen-acre ranch. Clarence Tharp, Ed's owner, would encourage mothers to bring their children over and watch Ed do tricks. The kids would ask Ed what two and two was, and Ed would stomp his hoof four times. Then he would open and close the barn door and wiggle his lips as if to talk.

Tahlequah resident Randy Gibson was a youngster then. He says, "I'm a huge Mister Ed fan. My mother actually knew Clarence Tharp, who trained Mister Ed and retired with him here when I was little. I remember seeing Mister Ed standing out in his field munching on grass a long, long time ago."

Wilma Bussy recalls Mister Ed, "He was the same nonchalant, easy-going personality of the television character. He was such a ham. He would mosey over and plant a kiss on the kids' cheeks with his big lips."

Ed made Tahlequah special. To this day its residents boast that Tahlequah is the final resting place of the most famous TV horse of all time.

The Pride of Tahlequah

Local lore is that Tharp, who was Mister Ed's trainer, purchased the horse at auction after the show's end in 1966. When Tharp retired to his daughter's home in Oklahoma in the late 1960s, he brought his prize show horse with him and proudly distributed his card, which read: "CLARENCE AND HIS EDUCATED HORSE, Mr. Ed—One of the World's Most Talented Horses—Open for Engagements."

The horse died in 1979 and was quietly buried. Tharp eventually passed away, and his daughter sold the property to Danny and Darlene Snodgrass. The unsuspecting young couple had no idea they owned a historic landmark until their new neighbors told them they used to visit Mister Ed there.

Tahlequah's memories of Mister Ed began to fade, until 1990 when two rubber-mouthed disc jockeys on 104.5 KMYZ-FM, Mel "Mel-in-the-Morning" Meyers and Steve "Banana" Bradley, caught wind of the story. They decided that Ed should have a grave marker and began a campaign to raise money to build a monument.

The dedication became a community event called "Edstock." The promoters painted horseshoe prints from the winding stretch of Highway 82 which lead to Ed's burial site on the Snodgrass Farm. Two hundred spectators gathered and a local band played "The Mister Ed Theme Song."

Tulsa television stations and all the newspapers around covered the event, which was broadcast live on Z104.5. A group of Girl Scouts laid a bouquet of carrots at the foot of the monument, which was engraved: "According to national media reports, Mr. Ed moved to Oklahoma in the late 1960's after a successful Hollywood career. Mr. Ed continued to entertain and bring joy to many Oklahomans, finally retiring in this very field. Mr. Ed passed away February 22, 1979. May His Memory Live Long."

Such fun was had by all that they made plans to do it every year as a kind of annual Ed-fest, and many new members were added to the Mister Ed fan club, the Ed-Heads.

The Movement Afoot (or ahoof) to Discredit Tahlequah's Mister Ed

But underlying the festivities were rumors—scandal—that the horse buried in Tahlequah was not the real Mister Ed. He might be an imposter. Reports out of Hollywood said Mister Ed had died ten years earlier in the San Fernando Valley.

It All Began...

The comedy show, *Mister Ed*, did not originate as a television series. It was a collection of magazine short stories written by Walter Brooks in *The Saturday Evening Post* and *Liberty*. The original Mister Ed could recite Shakespeare and speak Latin. But he also had some off-putting characteristics—he drank a great deal and was a carouser.

There were twenty-eight stories which director Arthur Lubin optioned for the TV series. Lubin had just sold his rights to his popular *Francis the Talking Mule* movies, and he wanted to translate the concept to television. He got George Burns involved. Burns put up the money for the original *Mister Ed* pilot, but it did not sell.

"The original horse ...was a pathetic-looking nag."

Alan Young, an established comedian who was chosen as head actor, frankly explained in his autobiography, *Mister Ed and Me*, "The original horse used in the pilot was a pathetic-looking nag. If the public was going to be attracted to Ed, he should be a fine-looking animal."

The Mister Ed Company then hired Lester Hilton, one of Hollywood's most accomplished animal trainers. As a young man, Lester had studied with, and worked for, the famous trick rider-comedian Will Rogers. Hilton had trained the talking mule in the *Francis the Talking Mule* movies for Universal. Young wrote, "They commissioned him to seek out the best-looking palomino stallion in Hollywood."

Within a week, Hilton found his star. His name was Bamboo Harvester, and Young described him as "a magnificent-looking palomino who had once belonged to the president of the California Palomino Society and had started out in life as a parade or show horse." He was born in El Monte, California, in 1949, and grew to be a beautiful stallion, ridden many times in the Rose Parade, just like his Grandsire, The Harvester. He was a natural "ham," accustomed to crowds and performing. Hilton paid $1500 for Bamboo Harvester and immediately began training him for shooting of the new series pilot, due in five weeks. From then on he was called Mister Ed.

From the Sublime to the Ridiculous

The *Mister Ed* show combined some of Hollywood's greatest talent—Willy Burns, George Burns' brother, and Norman Paul had been writers for *Burns and Allen*. Lou Derman, head writer, later worked on Norman Lear's *All in the Family* sitcom. Ed's make-up artist, Jack Pierce, was famous for creating the Frankenstein monster, Igor.

Mister Ed was an immediate hit. Unlike the sugary-sweet animals, such as Lassie, which were popular in the 1960s, Mister Ed was a cynical character. He could be jealous. He had opinions, and he had his moods. He liked to party all night and sleep till noon. He would feign illness to get out of doing something he found distasteful. Once he phoned the SPCA to complain about his treatment. And he constantly got Wilbur into jams.

Ed was thoroughly modern, expecting Wilbur to install central heating in his stall. He parked at the meter when he came to town. He could dance the twist, although he had difficulty getting his front end to coordinate with his back end. He styled his mane, and went on diet and exercise kicks. He read with glasses and did crossword puzzles.

Ed was also talented. He played harmonica and drums, ping pong, and basketball. In the most famous segment of all, he hit a home run at Dodger Stadium, then ran the bases.

And, he was adventurous. He went to Hawaii and rode a surfboard, then threatened to stay on and become a beachcomber. He loved to dally with the fillies, but wanted to get married some day.

Ed's guest stars were some of Hollywood's finest talent: Mae West, Clint Eastwood, Sharon Tate, and Zsa Zsa Gabor.

More Confusion than a Fugitive in the
Witness Protection Program

The show ran from 1961 to 1966 on CBS, then went into reruns. This is the point where the Hollywood and Tahlequah versions of the story begin to diverge. Hollywood sources say, after the show the studio paid Ed's expenses to live out his life with his trainer, Lester Hilton. Alan Young wrote that Ed eventually died and was cremated in Los Angeles and Lester died a few months later.

Jaine Nicolaides, who knew the horse throughout his entire life, is quoted in *The Famous Mister Ed*, "At the age of 19 [1968], Ed began having kidney problems, along with arthritis, and [had] trouble getting up and down in his stall." The vet said he would only worsen with time. All involved decided it would be best to put Ed to sleep.

Nicolaides claimed, "The news was not released to the press [because] the series was still being seen all over the country and many a youngster would have been deeply saddened if they knew the lovable horse they were watching was actually dead."

Shysters in These Here Parts

Alan Young addressed the issue of the horse buried in Oklahoma, "I read of the people in that area raising a fund to erect some sort of monument to his memory. [...] I found it difficult to shatter their illusions."

Young speculated, "The only possible explanation for this false report was that in 1960, before the show started, Filmways, the studio which filmed the series, shot some publicity stills, using a rented palomino. Later it was learned that after the show's success someone, possibly the one who rented Filmways the horse, was showing his animal around the country as the original Mister Ed." Young surmised this was the horse that died in the Midwest.

Loretta Kemsley, who grew up across the street from Mister Ed's stable and sometimes helped Hilton train him, denies he would have sold Ed to anyone. "Les was a wonderful man who loved his horses deeply, more than he did people. His love for Ed surpassed the love he had for all the other horses he worked with. It was in his nature to take care of Ed rather than urge the corporation to sell him off. If the corporation were to have offered him for sale, Les would have bought him rather than take the chance he'd be subjected to mistreatment."

She says there is an unverified story that a palomino in Oklahoma was hired for publicity purposes at a time when Ed was in California and not available. She suggests, "That is probably the palomino in Clarence Tharp's claim."

A Sordid Tale of a Horse Bamboozle

Kemsley speculates on an even more repugnant possibility, "It is common to use doubles for movie horses, especially 'star' horses who are too valuable to take a chance on injury. However, it is also common for horse traders who are shysters to make false claims about the horses they are trying to sell. It's sad how many people are duped but very common. Mr. Tharp could have genuinely believed he'd purchased Bamboo Harvester. Or, he could have known the horse was a double but still believed he was making a valid claim because of the publicity work. Or, he could have known this was just a palomino who looked like Mister Ed and made a false claim for reasons that made sense to him."

Let's Not Jump to Any Hasty Conclusions

Talequah residents are proud to claim Mister Ed as their most famous resident, deceased or not. But, do they have the right to their boastfulness? True, there seems to be a horse buried in Tahlequah, lying beneath a granite marker which announces, in essence, "Here lies Mister Ed." The horse's trainer, Lester Hilton, was from Oklahoma, he studied under Will Rogers, and he visited Oklahoma during the time he was caring for Mister Ed.

Mel Meyers, one of the DJ's who helped raise money for the Mister Ed grave marker in 1990, says today:

"In the end, when all is said and done, I came out believing it probably was not Mister Ed. The show's franchise called us from California and threatened us. They warned us to stop promoting the gravesite. They said it wasn't the real Mister Ed. We asked, 'If this isn't Mister Ed, where is he?' They didn't know. They had lost track of him, put him out to farm, Elmers Glue, who knows. They couldn't tell us where he was. They were planning to do a Mister Ed movie and didn't want news released about him being buried anywhere.

We tried so hard to verify that the Tahlequah horse was the real Mister Ed, but we couldn't. The owner, Mr. Tharp, had died, and the family was reluctant to verify it was Mister Ed.

So what was the harm? He was a fabulous horse. It was a tribute to Mister Ed, wherever he was. It was a good time, good publicity."

Mister Ed: "I always thought I'd end up in that great big prairie in the sky."

Residents of Tahlequah feel they have a significant historic landmark. Randy Gibson of the Chamber of Commerce would like to repaint the horse hooves on Highway 82, freshen up the monument, and mention Mister Ed in the city's promotional materials. Darlene Snodgrass still owns the property and enjoys the occasional visitors who come to pay their respects.

With the series still playing on cable, Mister Ed is as popular as ever. There is a good possibility the horse in question did have some connection to the show— he was a star any way you look at it. And Tahlequah is where the world comes to pay homage to Mister Ed...wherever he may be.

Feature Magazine Articles
Honorable Mention

Misery in Babb Switch
by
Trudy Graham

On Christmas Eve eighty years ago, misery and a little mystery struck the small Oklahoma town of Babb Switch. While most memories can be wonderful or terrible, individual or collective, the one which haunted an entire generation was the horror of one terrible night at their small school in 1924.

Babb Switch School sat on near-pasture land close to the tiny town of Babb Switch two miles west and six miles north of Roosevelt in Kiowa County in southwest Oklahoma. A one-room school building, just 24 by 36 feet, it had a single entrance/exit at the front. On a normal school day it housed one teacher—Mrs. Florence Hill—and 15 pupils ranging in age from six to near teens.

On the cold night of December 24, 1924, the small frame building was crammed to capacity. The teacher, the students, their parents and siblings, along with a few aunts, uncles and grandparents gathered for the annual Christmas program.

The bright colors of humble farm Christmas finery provided most of the room's decoration. The aroma of closely-packed humanity blended with the rich and spicy scent of the lovingly stuffed mesh stockings filled with big oranges, hard candies and nuts for each child.

A pine Christmas tree stood at the innermost end of the room, decorated with cut-out figures and paper chains, all handmade by the Babb Switch students.

Gifts for the children lay under the tree, brought by those same parents, and ablaze on the tree were dozens of white candles, their flames supplying the light for the cozy Christmas setting. Carols were planned, and after a word or two from a couple of local ministers the children would be rewarded with their stockings and gifts.

The joyous celebration was underway when the flame of one small candle touched a pine branch, sparking a chain reaction that would ignite an inferno.

The tree had been standing for several days and was dry as tinder. It was consumed in mere moments, the fire spreading to the gifts and then to the walls and roof. Last it found the terrified people scurrying to escape through the single door at the front of the small building.

A few attempted to survive by breaking the two small windows on either side of the single room, but their actions allowed a fresh rush of oxygen to fuel the flames. Hope of escape through the windows was crushed by the realization that heavy wire netting had been nailed to the outside, a measure adopted months earlier to prevent the entrance of vandals.

The mass exodus was thwarted by a door that opened inward and the bodies of the terrified simply stacked one on the other, the smallest of them at the bottom of the pile. The screams of the dying and the howl of the fire mingled in the December air.

It didn't take long, an estimated three minutes, for the building to be completely consumed. Since the building was built entirely of wood, in a short time all that was left were smouldering ashes atop the foundation stones. The few survivors who made it out of the building stared at the destruction in horror. Someone ran to a buggy, whipped the horse into action, and raced to Hobart, some seven miles away, to seek help.

While little could be done in the dark of the cold night, those who were still alive were rushed to Hobart hospitals to be treated for their burns. At dawn, the grisly task of identifying the dead began. Neighbors and friends spent Christmas day in this grisly task, often identifying whole families. Although the victims at the top of the heap had been burned most severely, usually a small article of clothing served as a clue.

Deeper in the pile some bodies were barely burned. These souls were killed by suffocation from crushing weight or the deadly smoke. The fire's toll reached 36 dead with 37 injured in hospitals, many in critical condition.

The news of the terrible Christmas Eve fire at Babb Switch reached many newspapers. Because of the widespread publicity, the event is credited as a major contributor to national legislation that restricted the use of candles on Christmas trees in public buildings and mandated all public schools have more than one entrance, doors that open outward, and unobstructed windows.

The Babb Switch Christmas Eve Fire is still listed on websites as one of the worst disasters of that era.

After a time, the school was rebuilt and used for a few years before the building was sold and moved to another community. Babb Switch became a ghost town. All that is left to mark the school's location is a tiny park with two picnic tables where the school once stood. A large granite marker on the site states:

SITE OF BABB SWITCH TRAGIC SCHOOL FIRE

On December 24, 1924, 35 people lost their lives while attending a Christmas party in a one-room frame school house. The fire was started by a candle on a Christmas tree. A school building was built here as a memorial and a model to point the way to safer county schools the nation over. The school was discontinued in 1943, was dismantled and sold.

It is interesting to note the discrepancy between the newspaper reports of 36 victims and the marker's reference to 35. Apparently, the 36th person was a four-year-old girl, assumed to have died in the fire although no body was recovered. She simply disappeared that night and was never found.

The survivors of that fateful night are long gone and their stories are remembered only fleetingly in the family stories of elderly relatives. While the details of that terrible Christmas are mostly forgotten, one part of the story lingers to this day. What happened to that little girl on Christmas Eve, 1924?

Primitive Art
by
Myrne Roe

He watched a hawk on a telephone pole, told Pete
Made the wife a chair for our anniversary. Made it
out of a galvanized tub, old tires. She saw it, went all quiet.
He examined the button she'd sewn on his coat sleeve.
Like she was choked up.

Pete nodded.

Same way when she got the yard cross I made out of old car bumpers.
He pushed his Farm Bureau cap forward
and scratched the back of his head.

Can't figure her out.
When she had the kid so fast I didn't get the coffee-can lamp made,
so I took her pink posies. She kissed me full on the mouth.

He watched the hawk swoop down on a sunny patch.
Found some old hubcaps and barbed wire. Her birthday's coming up.
I got me an idea for a decoration in her kitchen.
The hawk rose, critter in its claws.

Pete nodded.

The Goose
by
Denise White

I watched the single strands of clouds,

mares' tails,

passing high above the towering pine,

Norwegian pine.

I recalled the gaggle of geese plus one

Canada goose

that couldn't quite catch up.

I watched her tread air, reset her compass, and fly

North.

The Widow's Farm
by
Victor LaBrott

useless cries unheard while pain swells

as do heads and pockets

until cries no more

or all is one

again

one is all or

no more cries until

heads and pockets do as

pain useless while cries unheard swell

The Night is Cold
by
Norm Rourke

The night is cold,

Stars shine in a clear sky

That once was gray heavy with snow.

And a dusting of snow lays frozen on brown grass.

Old wood frame windows crack as cold settles in.

Food scraps put out for nocturnal critters

Lay stone hard in a terra cotta tray;

Only the brave—or foolish—will be out tonight.

Dens and nests shelter fur and feathers

Hunkered together for body heat warmth.

Winter comes hard to the southern plains

With nothing to stop the rush of Arctic air.

Ain't nuthin' holdin' it back between here

'n the North pole,"

Old timers say as they seek weather council

In wooly worms and persimmon seeds.

Every winter is the worst in memory.

And summer soon follows with its own claim.

But tonight's stars are bright,

A growing moon flashes on the snow field,

And covers feel warm as a den of sleeping bears.

Kodak

by
Carol K. Muirhead

frames outside my window
winter white and black
scrub oak vintage, tin-type print
cramp-on boulder, blowing grass
cacti clinging to the soil
that fickle rain
once kissed, and passed

bobcat refuge, tufts of brush
rocks of tannish gray
deer that camouflage their flesh
in holey crags, of pebbled suede

frozen landscape since early fall
when dying pods, spewed seeds to spoil
nothing moves, but arid sunshine
sculpting shadows of ancient Ute

tableau outside my window
ponderosa high
red fox, magpie, squirreling habit
where man can bare his soul to God

or sear his flesh in blazing heat
freeze his limbs in blizzard sleet
submerge his frame in dark room waters
where ocean seas…
once moved and flashed
Kodak frames…now catch…and last.

Novella ~ First Place

The Wager
by
Don Ballew

"Isn't this an absolutely gorgeous day?" Wanda McClamore purred as Theodore Lemons came into the office from the back entrance.

Assistant Coach Theodore Lemon's secretary greeted him with the same bubbly enthusiasm each morning, which was nice, but he wished she would occasionally assume the gloomy posture of the rest of the staff. It was tiresome, her being all smiles and full of cheer every living moment. Couldn't she see how difficult the football season was going to be at Western?

The sky was a crisp blue and the mountains surrounding the campus were showing their late summer colors. It truly was a beautiful morning but Lemons gruffly answered, "I never noticed," as he made a beeline for the cubicle that held the coffee pot.

"I got some news that's bound to get you perked up." Wanda continued her good-natured bantering.

"I bet," the grouchy coach answered. Can't that woman see that she just makes things worse?

"We just got another football player."

"You're not going to put me through that again," mumbled Lemons.

"You'll like this one. Said he'd be waiting outside in his pickup. Boy, is he ever cute," Wanda quipped, undaunted by the coach's gloom. "Said it was cold in here. Wasn't wearing much."

Lemons mental image of cute was a bowlegged runt. He hated the thought of the kind of specimen willing to bolster the sagging fortunes of the Western University football program. He ambled outside carrying his coffee mug, expecting the worst.

He easily spotted the pickup. It was the most battered vehicle he had ever seen outside of a junkyard. Completely out of sync, it had a fancy set of wide track tires with Mag wheels. Soft music emanated from expensive sound equipment, and it had velour bucket seats. Eons ago, the truck had been green. All the dents showed, with a few welds along the fenders, but it was gloriously waxed and polished. The door on the driver's side was open.

Lemons stopped looking at the battered truck and started to size up Wanda's latest recruit. The young man slouched on the running board with his head leaning against the seat, barely hanging on his narrow perch.

"He's wearing them snotty looking dark glasses. Man can't tell if they are paying attention or not. I just hate those gol durn things." Lemons mumbled.

When the youth noticed Lemons approaching he jumped up quickly and turned off the music, a gesture that pleased the coach. *At least he knows enough to show respect*, the coach thought.

"Hi." Lemons stretched out a hand. "Coach Lemons."

"Sir, I'm Elmer, Elmer Close."

"My secretary said you want to go out for our football team."

"That's right, sir."

"You finished high school?" Coach Lemons asked.

"Yes, sir."

"You ever been hurt?"

Lemons was trying to gauge what stood before him. He hated the sloppy appearance of cut-off jeans but at the moment, he didn't mind. The cut-offs let him see the knees. Being a hardened recruiter, he looked for the tell tale scars of the surgeons scalpel. The young man had none.

"No, not really. I jammed my neck swimming one time," replied Elmer Close. "I was about ten, maybe."

Lemons couldn't keep from marveling at the kid. He could make the team on looks. The coach, usually undaunted by the sight of talent, rummaged through his mind trying to think of what to do next. Football players worth anything didn't just show up out of the blue. They had all been looked at and heard about and the really good ones, the blue chippers, were written up in newspapers and magazines.

He listened to the kid's story, where he came from, all about his truck, then extremely suspicious, decided he ought to test Close some way, to see if he moved like a dry creek or the speed of light. Everyone needed speed. Lemons couldn't just tell the head coach they had "another" player. He needed to know more first.

"Let's go out on the field and see how you move. You feel like doing a little running?"

Lemons, trying to maintain his composure, had never seen anyone who looked as strong as this young man. Something had to be the matter with him. He wanted to find out what it was, before anyone else on the staff saw him.

"I'm right behind you," said Elmer Close.

The coaching staff at Western State University had, without knowing it, assumed the stance that nothing good could possibly happen to their organization. The NCAA had handed Western State severe penalties, but let them continue to play football. They would not be allowed to have a game televised for two years and no scholarships for one year. They could not recruit a single player. Walk-ons would have to fill the slots. Whoever heard of that! One year Kansas State had lost fifteen of their scholarships but not all thirty. The most damaging blow occurred when twenty-two freshmen and sophomore players were declared ineligible. Sixteen of them had been starters. The NCAA ripped the heart out of a mediocre (four and seven) football team. It would have been easier if they had been given the same treatment as Southern Methodist University and not allowed to compete for a few seasons.

The penalties had all been caused by the activities of over-zealous alumni and boosters. Sugar daddies, slush funds, ticket scalping, illegal jobs, cars…and the list went on. The coaching staff, except for two junior assistant coaches, had come out of the investigation unscathed. They jokingly told themselves they were now into character building.

The scheduling of football games, which in some cases was done years in advance, had projected Western State University where they wanted to be— division one, the big time. This early scheduling often created some horrible mismatches.

Western State's schedule had their season opening with the pollsters number one rated team, Oklahoma. The next week they faced the number three rated team, Alabama, and the following week the pollsters number two rated team, Pennsylvania State. All the games were away. The rest of their schedule included some of the Western Athletic Conference schools, and then they tapered off with University of Southern California and Arizona State, perhaps the toughest schedule of any team in the country.

Western had made the big time.

Maurice Weldon, the head coach, had not been fired but often wished he had. His constant companion was a bellyache, and for the most part retreated into his air-conditioned office. He had always been a winner, an optimist, and a creator of enthusiasm. Lately he said he wanted to vomit when he thought of taking his tiny band of warriors to Owen Field in Norman, Oklahoma.

Coach Lemons and the new prospect ambled onto the practice field.

"You won't need much warming up in this weather. Better a little though; I wouldn't want you to pull something. When you get loosened up, go down to the goal line and I'll time you to the forty. That's how we time football players. When I bring my arm down, I'll hit the watch."

Holy moley! He must have a rocket up his ass! thought Lemons as Elmer Close blasted out of his starting stance and an instant later crossed the forty-yard marker. Lemons had never seen anyone run a four-two forty before.

"Hey! How fast have you been doing the forty, kid?" Lemons asked, trying to remain calm. But he couldn't, his skin quivered from his ears down to the middle of his back.

"I been right around four-three for most of the year now. But right then, I kind of leaned on it."

Close, taking slow, deep breaths, was obviously in good condition.

You kind of leaned on it! "You want to show me how you can do the hundred?"

"Oh yeah! I can do that pretty good, too."

Lemons watched again in disbelief as the graceful young athlete moved toward him at world class speed.

"You just did a nine-two. You out here just showing off and you do a nine-two. How come I haven't heard about you before? You must be, what? Six-six? What do you weigh?"

"Two-seventy."

"Six-six and two-seventy," Lemons mumbled.

"Can you keep what we are doing between you and me and the head coach?" asked Close.

"How come?" Lemons asked, as they went back toward the building that housed the coaching staff. Maybe he's got something to hide, thought Lemons.

"I don't want to get started on the wrong foot with the rest of the guys. Let's just surprise the opponent with it."

"You're a welcome sight, son. I don't know what you're doing here. You must like it tough. I'm sorry to treat you like I did. You know, suspicious like, but we haven't had too many good things happen. Most of the guys who've shown up here lack something. We're glad to have them, don't misunderstand. We just need a lot more talent considering the schedule we have. You stay here by the truck. I don't want you cooling off too quick. I'll hunt up Coach Weldon."

Lemons found the coach sipping some Maalox in his office. He walked him to the window so he could get a look at Elmer Close. They stood peering down at the muscular youth, who wore a tank top with "Mooseville" written on the front and back.

"See the boy leaning against the green pickup? That's a six-six by two-seventy that does a four-two forty and a nine-two hundred. I just clocked him." Lemons was bursting with pride over his newfound recruit.

"Bullshit," Coach Weldon said. "Nobody ever done a four-two. That's a myth. Bo Jackson might have got close. What's wrong with him?"

"There isn't anything wrong. It's weird. This is the fastest, strongest-looking human I've ever seen, and he just shows up out of nowhere. Says you might be needing some help. He knows he has to pay his own way right down the line."

"Where is Mooseville?" Weldon asked.

"That's probably some sort of a nickname for his hometown. I never asked him about it. He's from a little town in Oklahoma called Deer City."

"Did you buy him the truck to get him to come here?" Coach Weldon asked, searching for some irony.

"I don't think they'll accuse us of that." Lemons was laughing more than usual at the head coach's attempt at humor. "He speaks of the rig almost with a reverence. It's a forty-six Ford half ton with a flat head six engine. He says it's part of the family. He opened the hood, made me look at the motor. Chrome blinded me—you could eat off it."

"Let's go and say hi to the kid."

Lemons and the coach headed toward the parking lot.

"Unreal," Lemons said. "And the closer you get, the stronger he looks. He seems to have his head screwed on unusually well for a kid. From the looks of things the NCAA can't give us any hell over him."

"Hi, Mr. Weldon. You folks have a nice campus." The new kid greeted them cheerfully.

"Hi, Elmer. Coach Lemons has been telling me about you. Do you have any questions about out program?"

"If I'm good enough, can I play on both teams?" Close asked. "Offense and defense?"

"I'd rather not plan on that," Weldon answered. "Too much for a player to learn."

"If I make it at nose guard, can I try out for quarterback? I can pass."

Coach Weldon did a double take toward Theodore Lemons then back at the kid. Lemons could practically read his mind—*Holy mackerel. He can pass, run and play defense. What the hell's going on here?*

"You know I can't mess around long with the schedule we have. I have to let the best man play, you know."

"I should be able to kick field goals, punt and kick off," Close added.

"We have three days before we open practice," Weldon said. "You can come down and work out with the people who are already here."

"I'll be there."

"Boy! He isn't short on confidence, is he?" Weldon asked Lemons as the young aspirant headed his truck toward the office of the registrar.

"Got plenty of that, all right."

The two men agreed they could be looking at real talent. Another peculiar aspect which both noticed, Close had the ability to dominate without being abrasive.

"He doesn't seem spoiled and snotty like a lot of the stars just out of high school. Too good to be true is maybe another set of words I'm looking for. I already like him and haven't seen him do anything except run. You know what I mean?" Lemons asked as he and Weldon went into the coach's office.

"I get that same feeling. He looks so clean. He's got all the confidence we're looking for. You look him in the eye and know there are no visible flaws. You'd bet good money he's okay. Same token, you just know there's got to be something the matter. With all the shit that's happened to us...Why would he show up here?" Weldon asked.

Both men had looked at Close in disbelief but weren't going to run him off. They certainly wanted him if he was as good as he looked. He could be a leader, although that seldom happened with freshmen. So far, they did not have anyone closely resembling a quarterback. The coaches still had difficulty believing their good fortune. A six-million-dollar man had just walked on.

They would rue the day they met Elmer Close Jr.

* * * * *

Elmer Close had grown up in unusually good circumstances. Not great wealth or any such thing; it was the love and warmth he shared with his family. He and his father were the best of friends. There was enormous love between them, and their personalities blended rather than clashed, as happens in most families. Both had a sense of humor, which spilled over into everything they did.

Close, Sr. idolized his son. He tried to not spoil the child but was continuously beside himself over his good fortune. While waiting for the child to be born, he'd wanted a son. More than anything, he'd wanted it to be healthy.

In the case of the Close child, there was never a prettier baby or more handsome son. And he was smart. Very bright. In fact, he gave the valedictory address. He was different than the other children in one noticeable way. He not only outgrew all his classmates at an early age, he proved to be so strong that he played competitive games with children much older. When he was ten, he could hold his own with fifteen-year-old football players.

By the time he entered junior high school his venture into sports was such an embarrassment of riches that they weren't fun to watch. The huge disparity inspired Elmer Close Sr. to play an enormous practical joke—a prank that would eventually lead Elmer Jr. to Western State University.

* * * * *

The father, a big, strong man himself, had discovered early that his son had strength beyond anyone's wildest imagination. When Elmer Jr. was in the eighth grade, he turned the junior high football season into a track meet. He was thirteen years old, 6'1" tall, weighed 191, and did the hundred yard dash in nine-six. Nearly every time he touched the football, he scored with it and was equally devastating playing defense.

"You keep playing like that and you'll be uncomfortable running over the other kids. How does this sound to you?" asked the father, as he began to unfold a game plan.

"To pull this off, you'll have to be an unknown athlete when you finish high school. You can play and practice, but keep a low profile. If you go and score forty points a game, you'll have every scout in the country breathing down your neck. You can play enough to win all your games. What you can do is act like you are hurt after the game is put away, and make sure your buddies get the glory plays. You will be noticed some, but if we work this right we can have you walk on to play football for the underdog in the biggest mismatch we can find at the start of the eighty-eight season. The big college coaches won't know you exist. You'll be a big, lazy kid who can't stand pain. You'll miss out on some honors in high school, but you can make up for that down the road.

"Hope you understand this is just a daddy's pipe dream. Heady stuff for a kid your age. With your size and speed you'll win lots of honors in sports. This is a private joke that will take four and a half years to pull off. What do you think? You interested?" the father asked.

Before Elmer Jr. could answer, the father continued, "You see, football, especially big college football, doesn't have a lot to do with school. I'm not sure where it fits in. Maybe somewhere in the entertainment business."

"Like you say, that's a long way off," Elmer Jr. answered. "Let me just play along and see what happens. Way it is now, our games don't amount to much. I can have a bunch of fun hanging around with the team and with other stuff. It sure would be fun to pull off a big upset. Never thought of college football as something to make a joke about. Might be, though."

"You'll get no pressure from me, whatever you do," Elmer Sr. said. "It's just a wild idea. How I happened to be married to your mother was weird, and then you came along. Makes me think someone is working miracles for me."

Elmer Jr. was already familiar with his unusual lineage. Elmer Close Sr. came from poor circumstances out of the Oklahoma Ozark Mountains. In 1955, when he was fifteen, he found out he could make sixty dollars a day working on a pipeline crew as a welder. That they worked seven days a week didn't bother him. His large size precluded anyone questioning he might not be the proper age. This was such a fantastic amount of money that when school started in fall he stayed on the job. He gave up school and family to follow pipeline construction. This meant moving every few months. At age eighteen he was six foot three inches tall and weighed 220 pounds. He was good-looking except for a scar across his left eyelid and cheekbone, caused from a fall against a woodstove when he was a toddler. The scarred, drawn, skin, gave him an angry expression. And he was self-conscious about it.

When Elmer Sr. was eighteen, he was welding in Saudi Arabia. Normally a shy person, he made a bold move which would affect him the rest of his life. He purchased a twelve-year-old girl at a slave auction. He was taken to the auction by a Saudi, a co-worker who had attended school in England. Elmer Sr. had been to farm auctions back home, but had never seen anything like this.

"Suppose I bought one? What would happen?"

"You would pay handsomely for it, and if it was a woman, you might have to fight to keep her on the way home. Some of the people here would steal her away from you to sell at another auction, and if necessary slit your throat."

"Suppose you bought one for me? How would that be?"

The agitated Elmer Close had noticed a tall, thin child for sale. When he saw the terror in the slave's eyes, he couldn't ignore the horror. Although he didn't want a slave or even a servant, he couldn't stand the thought of that poor creature becoming a slave. It didn't matter what sex the child was, either way it was wrong.

"What do you want?" his friend asked.

"See that kid over in the little cage?" Elmer replied. "It's not tied up, but they got it in a cage like some animal. We can't let it get hauled off like that. Not if I can help it. Look at the fear in those eyes."

"Are you crazy?" Mossed Kahed asked. "That's a girl. How much money do you have on you? She looks bad now, but still would bring a good price at another auction. See that big fat sheik with all the people around to wait on him? Bet he bids on her. She'll go into his harem."

"I got seven hundred and sixty dollars with me in your kind of money. You can bid up to the end of that for me, anyway. If that's not enough, it's not enough." Close was frantic with his demands that Kahed bid on the child.

"I don't think you know what you are getting yourself into."

The bidding for the young girl stopped at $460. The fat sheik was, in fact, the chief bidder, but had already made several other purchases. He had little interest in the emaciated young girl. Close suddenly owned another human.

Kahed had advised Close before they went to the auction that it was a dangerous place. He said Close, himself, was excellent slave material and should carry a knife and gun.

"Uncover your forty-five and have your hand on it. This is no time to be polite," Kahed said to him as they went to collect their merchandise.

Close kept an angry eye on everyone as he and the Saudi made their way out of the auction without incident. The young girl urinated on herself as they approached the filthy cage.

"Shit," Close muttered in disgust.

He all but ripped apart the cage to free her, his heart breaking for the little girl. They sat her in the front seat of the Jeep with Kahed close behind, to make sure she would not run away. Although there was no place to go, animal fear could cause her to do something foolish.

Close couldn't understand why he felt so compelled to take on this burden. He was in a foreign country. Even if he could communicate with her, taking care of a child was a huge responsibility.

"Kahed, ask her where she's from. Maybe we can take her home."

The young girl apparently sensed she had nothing to fear from the big man, and fell asleep. She stayed with Kahed and his wife. Close came often. He obtained books from the American school and began teaching her.

As she began to speak, he learned she had been captured in a war. What war? He wondered. The big one was over in 1945; the Korean War was in another direction. He learned she had been part of a caravan that was filled with people leaving the war zone. The girl had been separated from her parents a long time ago, and she had traveled far.

"There are people who look like her in the Red Sea area," Kahed told Close.

The two years Close stayed in Arabia went by quickly and uneventfully. The Kaheds convinced him to take the girl to the United States. If she stayed in Arabia, she would have few opportunities and could become a slave again. She had grown three inches in height and was on the verge of becoming a beauty.

Since she could only get a passport if she married an American, Close and the Kaheds convinced themselves it was in her best interests. Kahed's wife posed as the young girl for a marriage ceremony, thus without her knowledge she became Elmer's bride.

In 1960, twenty-year-old Elmer and fourteen-year-old Rachael arrived in the United States. He enrolled Rachael in a boarding school for girls in Kansas City. He called her often, they wrote to each other, and he visited whenever he could. His work took him all over the United States and twice to South America, but she was always in his thoughts.

Rachael won many honors in school and developed into a beautiful young lady. Her perfect smile and delicate olive skin made her quite striking—especially since she was six feet tall and perfectly proportioned.

Close was hopelessly in love with this gorgeous creature, but he suffered in silence, certain she would never find him attractive. She was becoming educated and he had little formal schooling. He had plenty of knowledge, but no diplomas to show for it. Each day he grew more certain that his part in her life would soon end. She was in her third year at the University of Kansas. He punished himself with the thought she would fall in love with someone more attractive and sophisticated.

He had never dared tell her of the clandestine marriage in Arabia. There had been no marriage, not to his way of thinking. He told her to use the Close name and to think of him as her guardian with no strings attached—it had been his pleasure to help her escape from slavery and his reward would be her future happiness.

At the end of Rachael's junior year in college, she visited Close on a job site near Kansas City. It rained and rained. Pipeline construction came to a halt while the crew waited for the ground to dry, giving the pair more time to spend together.

One day Rachael and Elmer were riding in his aging Ford pickup truck, looking at the work site. Suddenly their conversation took an intimate turn. "What do you plan to do with your life after you finish school?" Close asked.

Almost as if she didn't hear his question, she asked, "Why have you never seemed interested in me as a woman? I'm not too young for you."

Although taken aback, Close replied, "Well, I suppose…fear of rejection. I've idolized you from the moment we hauled you away from the auction. Can you possibly understand I didn't want to do anything to cause us to break up our relationship…such as it is?"

"You mean you haven't expressed your true feelings because you're afraid I might tell you to bug off?"

"Yeah. That's about it."

"We're wasting time, big guy," Rachael said. "You're the only man I ever think about in the real love sense."

All those years of touching, saying good-bye, or hello, and they had never kissed. At once he was embracing her, his tears falling on her soft black curls. The big, tough construction foreman was crying. He was ecstatic.

In 1967, they changed their Arabic marriage license for one made in the USA. Rachael didn't return to college. The only child they would have came in the summer of 1970—a thirteen-pound son.

The Closes stopped their nomadic life the year Elmer Close Jr. was ready to start school. They settled down on a 320-acre farm near Deer City, Oklahoma. Elmer planned to farm and run a machine shop to supplement his income. The machine shop became such a good business the farm business was forgotten.

Large drilling rigs came to the Deer City area to plunge drill pipe five miles deep into the earth in search of natural gas. By the 1980s, Close employed twelve men.

In what seemed like a heartbeat, Elmer Close Jr. was on the high school football team. He was big and fast but rarely carried the football. Instead, he played quarterback on offense and nose tackle on defense. He enjoyed his father's plan to stay out of the limelight.

The Deer City football team won 52 games in a row and garnered four straight class AA championships. Close was noticed by some of the college scouts. Anyone as big and strong, had to be spotted. He never ran at full speed so the scouts did not see that side of him. His ability to get out of a game after it was put away was a good acting job. He either had leg cramps, or a muscle pull, or even a headache when he ran. The team always won. With the talent they had, the coach did not worry too much about Elmer Close, Jr. Of course, he had no knowledge of their far-fetched game plan. Just like everyone else, he was easily manipulated.

Close, Sr. had been adamant about scouts. "I don't want them scouts giving my boy the big head. You tell them I'm one of the meanest bastards you ever saw and the kid couldn't care less about winning."

"Why you want to do that to the boy? He is kind of crippled and gets cramps a lot, but he might win a scholarship somewhere. If I talk down to the recruiters, he won't get much of anything."

A few recruiters attempted to visit the Close family but not for long. The big man with the angry eye intimidated them. Many of Elmer's less talented teammates went to major universities on athletic scholarships.

* * * * *

Since the Western State University coaching staff had never heard of Elmer Close, Weldon called Deer City's coach. "I'm sorry to bother you this late. I'm Maurice Weldon. I coach football at Western State University and we had a peculiar thing happen today. We had a walk on from your school named Elmer Close. He looks like one hell of a prospect. Our situation is so hopeless with our schedule, we'll take anything. What can you tell me about the kid?"

"Well, that's a curious one you have there. I always wondered what happened to him. Never seen anybody put together that good. I felt like he gave about one percent of his ability here. He's smart and knows a lot about football. A true team player, always cheering the other kids. I enjoyed coaching him. His dad asked me to steer recruiters away, like they wanted to hide. If he ever decides to do anything, he ought to be a dandy. I can't figure what he's doing at Western. The NCAA really mopped up you guys, didn't they?"

The conversation with the high school coach only left Weldon with more questions. He had a big, fast player and would simply have to wait and see.

The first day in full pads Close began to dominate. They had to pull him from defense before he killed what was left of the offense. Yes, he could play nose tackle all right. Football is a hitting game, and he hit everyone. First he flattened the center, then anyone who posed as a blocker, and the poor ball carrier really got it.

Close started as quarterback. Head coach Weldon was astonished at his abilities—the lad could throw the long ball and was very accurate at any length pass needed.

The young giant, in a smooth and unobtrusive manner, began to take charge of the Western offense. He suggested to Coach Lemons that they use the old spread formation some of the time. With the talent they had, it might be possible to get more from that than the conventional "I" formation.

"Where'd you hear about that?"

"I've read lots of books about football," Close said.

"The play was used before you were born. We could try it. Only a tailback like you could successfully run it."

79

Coach Weldon hunted his play-books from the fifties and began to experiment with the spread formation. The boy was correct—the spread was perfect for them.

The other players soon realized they were playing football with someone special. When the players came to practice on the first day, they knew they were destined to lose for eleven straight Saturdays, but Close's abilities soon began to build team confidence. He threw the ball extremely hard, and, in time, the receivers learned the rockets were going to be on the numbers if they made the correct cut.

Once the skilled-handed players got accustomed to the ball coming at them like a missile, they liked the advantage it gave them over the defenders. Close could also toss the ball softly if necessary. And when he decided to run the ball, he was a marvel to watch.

Coach Weldon decided to close his practices to the press after two sessions. He didn't want them needlessly raising the hopes of fans. Western still had problems, even with the Close kid on hand. He also didn't want Oklahoma getting ready for the spread, especially a spread formation run by 'his' tailback.

* * * * *

Elmer Close Sr. and his son visited almost daily by phone, and, naturally, they talked about what was happening with the football team. The son kept insisting they would represent themselves very well. The father called the Monday before Saturday's game at Norman to unveil a new twist to his grandiose scheme.

"If this works out like it has in the past, the betting odds will be big as they can get. I, you will notice I said I and not we, can put some money down at the casinos. If we win, we could walk off with a bundle. Since you're the only kid in the family you'd have a stake in the game. Of course, we would never admit that to anyone. Got to keep you pure as the driven show," Elmer Close Sr. said. There was a pause on the other end of the line.

"You mean you're going to bet on us in the game against Oklahoma?" the son asked.

"If you think it's okay. You know what I mean. You'll have to decide what the team attitude is and also have to judge whether your bunch can play and stay hooked up against the Sooners. I'll call again before I do anything," his dad replied.

"I'll have think it over. You really caught me off guard," Close Jr. said.

Since the Western State University football team would leave Friday for their Saturday game at Norman, Close Sr. called his son again on Thursday.

They chatted for a while and Close Sr. asked the big question, "How you think your bunch is going to do?"

"We're going to be okay. We lack size. You've heard the old cliché—we're small but slow. Most of the guys stayed. Coach Weldon gave us hell during the three-a-days and the two-a-days, you know, he gave everyone plenty of reason to quit, but the guys stayed. One way they're scared, you know, over the schedule and another way, it's a challenge. Everybody who stayed has humped up and hustled.

Most of them think we'll get a licking at OU. I feel with a break or two we can do better. They'll be hard to beat but I'm playing both ways." Close Jr. exuded confidence.

"You don't think Western will give up?"

"I'd be surprised."

"You're going to be running the offense the whole time?"

"Unless I get wounded or we run up the score," Close answered with a snicker.

* * * * *

The Close family dined together in the Downtown Sheraton Hotel where the team was staying in Oklahoma City. As they ate, the father explained, "OU is favored by forty-six on the point spread. I've put a hundred and ten thousand on Western on those odds. That's to cushion the next bet. I got ninety-nine to one when I bet on Western to win. I put a hundred and ten thousand on that. Doesn't sound like the careful person I've been all my life, does it?" Close Sr. asked with a nervous grin.

Elmer Close Jr. turned pale and stared at this father in disbelief. After he recovered, he began to scribble on a napkin.

"My God!" he whispered. "If we win that's eleven million dollars. Years ago, when you talked about this, I had no idea you were planning something so big. It'll damn sure make the game more exciting."

"I never counted on the money part until recently. You see, the way I figure it, we won't miss any meals, even if I lose my whole wad. Give them hell, but don't hurt yourself. Going to be hot out there. As you can guess, I've done a lot of rationalizing to justify my behavior. Most people live their whole lives and won't ever get a shot at something like this. I'll survive one way or the other."

* * * * *

Good afternoon, sports fans. It's football time again in Norman, Oklahoma, home of the Oklahoma Sooners. Today we open the nineteen-eighty-eight football season for the Big Red. This is Marcus Coleman speaking to you on the Oklahoma football network. We wish to welcome two new radio stations, KRUA in Anchorage, and KGUM on the island of Guam. We have also been chosen to be on the armed forces network this week. Today's game will be broadcast around the world.

You can no doubt hear 'Boomer Sooner' being played by the OU band, The Pride of Oklahoma. This is the twenty-third straight sell out crowd at Owen Field.

As you probably know, OU is heavily favored in today's game. They have been picked by the pollsters to be the national champions of college football. They are featuring the world's fastest human, Milford Bruner, who won the hundred-meter dash in the recently held Olympics. He is a senior from Twitty, Texas, and a leading candidate for the Heisman Memorial Trophy. It was a question as to whether he would return to school or go on the world amateur track circuit. The lure of perhaps winning the Heisman trophy brought him back to school."

Another outstanding player pro scouts will be watching is Harold Prather. He made the All-American team last year as offensive center and hails from Westville,

Oklahoma. Prather, a two-hundred-and-eighty-pounder, is proud to call himself a Cherokee Indian.

It is a hot day. The temperature at game time is one hundred and four degrees with a twenty-five mile an hour wind, and the temperature on the playing field could reach almost one hundred and thirty degrees. The stamina of the players will be sorely tested.

Western State has won the toss and elected to take the wind. They will kick off from the south end.

The Western squad has Elmer Close, a freshman from Deer City, Oklahoma, kicking off. He approaches the ball, the crowd is on its feet, and the game is underway.

There will be no run back. Close kicked the ball into the stands. He looks like quite a kicker. Although there is a strong wind, he really put his foot into the ball. The ball is being placed on the twenty. With this hot wind, most of the balls kicked off from the south end, the open end of the stadium, will be kicked into the north stands.

Oklahoma is out of the huddle. The quarterback, Bolger, is under the center. He hands off to the first man through, the fullback, Masters, who is blasted hard for a one-yard loss. The tackler is number sixty-one, Elmer Close—the player from Deer City who kicked off.

Oklahoma tried to utilize their big center, Harold Prather. Close is the nose tackle for Western, and he slipped between Childs, the left guard, and Prather to flatten Masters. Masters is leaving the game hunched over holding his side. We hope he is not seriously injured.

Down number two. Bolger is down under. He spins to his left, goes down the line of scrimmage and pitches to Milford Bruner. Bruner makes his turn up field and is hit hard by number sixty-one, Elmer Close. Milo Prinsor of Western took out two blockers from Bruner. This Close kid gets around pretty good for a big man. Oklahoma lost another yard. Looks like number sixty-one, Close does nearly everything on defense. He's a freshman and he's calling the defensive signals.

Third and twelve. Bolger down under, he spins to his right and finds a crack between end and tackle and squirts through for five yards. That run looked more like Oklahoma offense we are used to. Bolger may have gotten a first down if they could have blocked the linebacker down on that side.

Krug, OU's punter, is standing on about the five yard line and will kick from the eight or nine. Western's decision to take the wind is paying off, as Western should get the ball on Oklahoma's side of the fifty.

He gets a good snap from center.

Oh my goodness! It's blocked! He caught it! He will score! Western has scored on Oklahoma! This is incredible! Number sixty-one, Elmer Close, flattened Prather, the Oklahoma center, and when he got close to the kicker, he launched himself to where he was towering high above Krug when he kicked. Close juggled the ball slightly and came down with it and trotted into the end zone.

Needless to say, the home crowd is stunned. I can't say enough to describe the agility the nose tackle from Western showed on that play.

The Western State team acted very businesslike in the first score. Instead of the usual display of enthusiasm that we normally see after most touchdowns, they've gone directly into their huddle and are now coming out for their extra point attempt.

The kicker, as you can probably guess, is Elmer Close. The kick is down and through the uprights, waaaayy up into the stands. The score is Western State seven and OU zero. We will be right back after this message...

The University of Oklahoma started on the twenty after the ball was kicked into the stands on the kickoff again. Oklahoma attacked with their vaunted wishbone, moving the ball only three yards in two plays. Bolger, OU's quarterback, went back to pass and had to throw the ball away because of pressure from the nose tackle, Elmer Close.

Krug, the punter, is standing on the eight to receive the snap from center. He has to be thinking about the last punt. Krug gets the ball in good shape. It's blocked! Incredible! Close of Western has blocked his second punt. Prather has not been able to handle him at all. He did not catch this punt, and it went out of bounds on the thirty-one of Oklahoma. The punt went eight yards from the line of scrimmage. Western has excellent field position.

We will now get a chance to see the Western offense after a message from our sponsor.

After a short break, Coleman was back.

They're coming out in a spread formation. I haven't seen this formation in a long time...maybe twenty-five, thirty-five years ago. Elmer Close is their tailback and passer! He's changing jerseys to play both ways. He is number one on offense.

Close receives the ball from the center at about the forty and fires it to Alfred Shore, who goes out of bounds after a six-yard gain. Oklahoma is using a three-man rush, and they hardly got past the line of scrimmage before the ball was thrown.

For those unfamiliar with it, the spread, for all practical purposes, has only one man in the backfield, and the rest of the offense is strung across the field along the line of scrimmage. It spreads the defense. It fell out of favor because teams had a tough time scoring from inside the twenty with it.

Down number two. Close catches the ball from center at about the thirty-four. He moves toward the line of scrimmage and again fires the ball to Shore down the middle. He is downed immediately on the sixteen. First down, Western. Shore looked like he was headed for the end zone and cut in front of the safety, leaving him wide open.

This Close kid looks like some kind of an athlete. We will be hearing a lot about him. The Western team is all business.

First and ten on the sixteen. Close catches the ball on the twenty-four and heads up field to his right. He is going to run. He is hit hard at the five and drags two Oklahoma defenders with him into the end zone. I am over using the word 'incredible,' but, I am stunned by this. Close has outstanding speed and runs with the power of two Earl Campbells. When he turned the corner at the ten, it looked like no power could possibly keep him out of the end zone. Kiser and Stacey both had him at the five, and he hardly broke stride. Western has exploded the myth that you can't score inside the twenty with the spread formation.

Western is lined up for the extra point. The ball goes directly to Close. They are going for two! They have two! Close moved toward the line like he was going to run, leaped high into the air, and flipped the ball to Glen Module standing in the end zone.

Western leads fifteen, zip. Next a message from our sponsor."

Typically, an underdog team playing OU could maintain an intense game for the first quarter. After that, the superior strength of the Oklahoma team became overwhelming and they enjoyed running up the score. It was always a good way to fatten their ratings.

The crowd sat in the burning sun, certain it would be only a matter of time before Milford Bruner broke loose for one of his long runs. Western had merely gotten lucky. The entire crowd was certain Western's time in the spotlight would be short. However, there was a fly in the ointment, a big one—Elmer Close. He had dominated the game from the early moments. Time and again the ball carrier left the field in pain as the heralded Oklahoma ground attack was met with savage force.

Western kicked off to OU, and the wishbone began to move. Western was grudgingly giving ground. The two-touchdown lead had built a fire under the Sooners. The first long OU drive, which took six minutes, was stopped on the twelve by a fumble. Western punted after only one successful first down. It went out of bounds on the Oklahoma twenty.

Oklahoma again fumbled the ball away on their own thirty. Close kicked a 42-yard field goal after three incomplete passes. Western eighteen, Oklahoma zero, as the first quarter came to a close.

How long would Elmer Close play both ways effectively in the intense heat? It was close to 130 degrees Fahrenheit on the playing field. Both teams were substituting continuously with the exception of Elmer.

Close Sr. was worried about his son. Years earlier he had sat on row two as OU played California when they had the courageous Roth at quarterback. During that sweltering game it was like sitting in the door of a huge furnace. Close knew his son was playing in the same kind of heat.

"I wish he'd take himself out," he told Rachael.

The game droned on through the second quarter with no Oklahoma score and Western State missing one field goal and making another. The spread formation was not a good formation for scoring, but Western was using it to perfection and controlling the ball.

The partisan Oklahoma crowd urged their team on.

The half-time score was announced across the nation, with Western State leading Oklahoma 21 to zip. All the sports junkies knew it was either a mistake or Oklahoma would correct the situation in the second half.

Oklahoma kicked off with the wind in the second half. Western took the ball on the twenty and used seven agonizing minutes of the quarter on a drive that ended with a missed field goal.

The Sooners finally scored late in the third quarter and again in the fourth quarter. The fans knew from then on it would be just a matter time. They would get to see the Big Red run. No one would keep Milford Bruner checked for a whole ball game. He was bound to break loose. The Western defenders were beginning to look tired. Actually they looked exhausted.

Ladies and gentlemen, the score is still Western twenty-one, Oklahoma fourteen. Three minutes and twenty seconds to play. The crowd has been yelling at the OU players to pull something out of the hat. Can the Close kid hold together long enough to finish the game? He is literally dragging between plays. I don't remember when I've seen a player look so exhausted. He has played every second of the game. I don't have enough superlatives to describe his performance today. I've never seen anything like it.

OU is out of the huddle. Second and eight on their own eighteen. Bolger is under the center. He spins left all the way around and pitches the ball to Bruner, who blasts through a big hole between right end and tackle. He may go! He is in the clear at the forty...fifty, forty, thirty, twenty. Close catches him and slams him to the turf on the seven. He really caught Bruner on the thirteen and knocked him to the seven.

I don't know if you can hear me or not. Elmer Close of Western State has just run down and tackled the world's fastest human. He had no angle. It was just an incredible feat. Our instant replay shows Close was down, tackled at the line of scrimmage. He got up and ran Bruner down. Bruner knew he was coming on and put everything he had into getting to the end zone.

Close is not getting up! He is on his knees with his hands on his hips, his head tilted back, and is gasping for air. He is signaling for a time out. We will be back after this message from our sponsor.

During the time out Close's teammates on the field asked if he was all right. He said he'd be fine after a breather. He stayed in the same position with his head back and his helmet off during the time out. He took another time out as soon as the first one was over, accepting the one-half the distance to the goal penalty.

Milford Bruner, the talented speedster, stood to one side and stared at Elmer Close. The expressions of his teammates reflected the same question. Had Bruner lost his world's-fastest-man title on the floor of Owen Field? Who was this guy? No doubt, the Oklahoma coach, who was supposed to know where all the good football players were, was asking his staff where Western found the sonnovabitch.

Close's father was in agony. He wanted his son out of the game. The fear that his son would hurt himself overshadowed all thoughts of money. "How come the coach doesn't pull him? Anybody can see he's worn out!" he yelled to Rachael.

Sooner's ball, first and goal on the three and a half. Bolger down under. Bolger cuts to his left and is flattened as he pitches to Masters on a sweep. Masters does not make it back to the line of scrimmage! He may have lost two yards. Close and company hurled him to the turf before he could get out of bounds.

The mighty Oklahoma offense was thrown back by the rag-tag Western defense for the next three downs. They ran two downs and attempted to pass on another. Bolger could not get the pass away and was swarmed under on the twelve yard line.

Close took the ball from the center for the next three downs and sat down as Oklahoma used all their remaining time outs. He caught the ball in the end zone, took a safety, then lifted a towering punt that turned over and landed out of bounds at OU's fifteen. Oklahoma had the ball on their fifteen with forty-two seconds remaining.

What a ball game! The temperature isn't the only thing hot today. Can OU pull this out with forty-two seconds on the clock?

Bolger is yelling the signals. He spins, pitches to Bruner on a sweep, and is run down before he gets to the line of scrimmage. It's Close again. I can't believe it! This man is much faster than Bruner. He has to be. He's shown it time and time again. Bruner did not get out of bounds, and they are getting ready to run another play. Bolger throws the ball out of bounds to stop the clock. Twenty-three seconds to play.

Bolger barks the signals. He is running back to pass, but he will never get it away. Big number sixty-one, Close, almost caught him before he moved away from the center. It was a race to see how far he could get before getting hurled to the turf. He lost six yards.

Oklahoma is hurrying to get a play off, six seconds, five, four...Bolger takes the ball from center and pitches to Bruner, and he bursts through the line of scrimmage for eight yards. The Western defense could not get him off his feet, but they had such a firm hold on him that the referee's whistle blew the play dead. Bruner is handing the ball to the official. The game is over, and the mighty Sooners have been beaten to the tune of twenty-one to sixteen!

We are witnessing an unusual gesture, ladies and gentlemen. The Oklahoma team has lined up to shake hands with Elmer Close. I think this is a gracious move on their part. I have never seen such an unbelievable performance. To totally dominate a ball game on offense and defense, as hot as it is, has to be a superhuman feat. What an outstanding freshman!

Elmer Close Sr. had never been interested enough in gambling to engage in the penny ante gin games at the local country club. He had placed his bets in Las Vegas sporting old wrinkled khaki clothes he had worn while welding. A few small holes were burned in the sleeves. His old cap, advertising Close Machine Shop, along with the khakis, made him appear poor and ignorant—just the demeanor he wanted to show. When he counted the eleven thousand dollars out in crisp new hundred-dollar bills, the casino attendants taking the bets felt sorry for the sucker.

"My boy plays for Western. He's real stout."

He returned to collect his winnings wearing an off-white, tailored pinstripe suit. A beautiful, olive-skinned woman was at his side. They looked intimidating, as he had hoped they would, as they collected $1,089,000 for each of his ten bets, plus the $100,000 on the other bet. His scam had worked. He took a terrible beating from the Internal Revenue Service, but still came home with a fortune. There would be no more stringer beads, and no more welding in muddy bell holes.

"What are you going to do now that your financial status has changed?" Elmer Jr. asked his father.

"I guess I'll get a plastic surgeon to fix my eye, and maybe me and Rachael will go on a search for her roots."

"Aw, Dad. Your eye looks fine to me, and it's dangerous to poke around where Mom's roots are," Elmer said, loving his parents exactly as they were.

HUGE BETTING SCANDAL ROCKS COLLEGE FOOTBALL!

The headline ran nationwide, followed by the story. The Nevada casino managers had yelled, "Fix" after discovering their accumulated losses. Inside the sports pages later in the week, the readers would find Elmer Close, Jr. had received a lifetime suspension from NCAA events for his part in the betting scandal. Theodore Lemons was banned for two years for improper recruiting, and Western State's football program would cease for three years, then forfeit two more years on television. In short, the school's dream of playing big time college football was history.

Elmer Close Sr. could not understand what anyone had done wrong. He had simply bet on his son, and won.